Compassion Focused Therapy

CW01082423

Research into the beneficial effect of developing compassion has advanced enormously in the last ten years, with the development of inner compassion being an important therapeutic focus and goal. This book explains how Compassion Focused Therapy (CFT)—a process of developing compassion for the self and others to increase well-being and aid recovery—varies from other forms of Cognitive Behaviour Therapy.

Comprising 30 key points this book explores the founding principles of CFT and outlines the detailed aspects of compassion in the CFT approach. Divided into two parts—Theory and Compassion Practice—this concise book provides a clear guide to the distinctive characteristics of CFT.

Compassion Focused Therapy will be a valuable source for students and professionals in training as well as practising therapists who want to learn more about the distinctive features of CFT.

Paul Gilbert is Professor of Clinical Psychology, University of Derby and has been actively involved in research and treating people with shame-based and mood disorders for over 30 years. He is a past President of the British Association for Cognitive and Behavioural Psychotherapy and a fellow of the British Psychological Society and has been developing CFT for twenty years.

Cognitive-behavioural therapy (CBT) occupies a central position in the move towards evidence-based practice and is frequently used in the clinical environment. Yet there is no one universal approach to CBT and clinicians speak of first-, second-, and even third-wave approaches.

This series provides straightforward, accessible guides to a number of CBT methods, clarifying the distinctive features of each approach. The series editor, Windy Dryden, successfully brings together experts from each discipline to summarise the 30 main aspects of their approach divided into theoretical and practical features.

The CBT Distinctive Features Series will be essential reading for psychotherapists, counsellors, and psychologists of all orientations who want to learn more about the range of new and developing cognitive-behavioural approaches.

Titles in the series:

For further information about this series please visit www.routledgementalhealth.com/cbt-distinctive-features

Compassion Focused Therapy

Distinctive Features

Paul Gilbert

Routledge
Taylor & Francis Group

LONDON AND NEW YORK

First published 2010 by Routledge
27 Church Road, Hove, East Sussex BN3 2FA

Simultaneously published in the USA and Canada
by Routledge
711 Third Avenue, New York NY 10017

*Routledge is an imprint of the Taylor & Francis Group,
an Informa business*

Typeset in Times by Garfield Morgan,
Swansea, West Glamorgan
Printed and bound in Great Britain by

This publication has been produced with paper manufactured to
strict environmental standards and with pulp derived from
sustainable forests.

British Library Cataloguing in Publication Data
A catalogue record for this book is available from the British Library

Library of Congress Cataloging in Publication Data
Gilbert, Paul, 1951 June 20–
    Compassion focused therapy : distinctive features / Paul Gilbert.
        p. cm.
    ISBN 978-0-415-44806-2 (hbk.) – ISBN 978-0-415-44807-9 (pbk.)
1. Emotion-focused therapy. 2. Compassion–Psychological aspects.
3. Cognitive therapy. I. Title.
    RC489.F62G55 2010
    616.89'1425–dc22

                                                2009046045

ISBN: 978–0–415–44806–2 (hbk)
ISBN: 978–0–415–44807–9 (pbk)

Contents

Preface and acknowledgements

I would like to thank Windy Dryden for putting this excellent series together, inviting me to contribute, and his patience with my various efforts to do so. I found it daunting because to date there is no major text on Compassion Focused Therapy (CFT), so there was a need for some background and evidence for the value of a compassion approach. In consequence this volume is a smidgen longer and more referenced than others in the series—so many thanks to Windy, Joanne Forshaw and Jane Harris at Routledge for all their support.

I have tried to indicate the distinctive features while at the same time recognizing the huge debt and borrowing from other approaches. Many thanks to all who have supported CFT especially my current research team: Corinne Gale, Kirsten McEwan and Jean Gilbert; the board members of the Compassionate Mind Foundation: Chris Gillespie, Chris Irons, Ken Goss, Mary Welford, Ian Lowens, Deborah Lee, Thomas Schroder and Jean Gilbert; clinical colleagues who have also been working on this approach, Michelle Cree, Sharon Pallant and Andrew Rayner, who have all shared their knowledge, insight and learning, greatly enriching our understanding of CFT. Gratitude goes to Giovanni Liotti who guided me in the importance of mentalizing and how to link that with social mentalities; to Andrew Gumley for his support, interest and leadership in the field of psychosis and to Sophie Mayhew and Christine Braehler for their inspiring CFT work with people with psychosis. Compassionate focused therapy is supported by the Compassionate Mind Foundation which offers links to other compassion focused websites and updates, downloads and training in CFT (see www.compassionatemind.co.uk). Thanks also to all those who contribute to the compassionate mind discussion list (also see www.compassionatemind.co.uk). My gratitude goes to Diane Woollands for her wonderful support in running the Compassionate Mind Foundation and Kelly Sims for her enthusiasm, secretarial work and reference checking—no small feat.

This book is dedicated with thanks to all the clients who over many years have shared their tragedies and triumphs and guided the development of CFT with their honesty of what helps and what doesn't. To all I owe a great debt.

Part 1

THEORY: UNDERSTANDING THE MODEL

Some basics

All psychotherapies believe that therapy should be conducted in a compassionate way that is respectful, supportive and generally kind to people (Gilbert, 2007a; Glasser, 2005). Rogers (1957) articulated core aspects of the therapeutic relationship involving positive regard, genuineness and empathy—which can be seen as "compassionate". More recently, helping people develop *self*-compassion has received research attention (Gilbert & Procter, 2006; Leary, Tate, Adams, Allen, & Hancock, 2007; Neff, 2003a, 2003b) and become a focus for self-help (Germer, 2009; Gilbert, 2009a, 2009b; Rubin, 1975/1998; Salzberg, 1995). Developing compassion for self and others, as a way to enhance well-being, has also been central to Buddhist practice for the enhancement of well-being for thousands of years (Dalai Lama, 1995; Leighton, 2003; Vessantara, 1993).

After exploring the background principles for developing Compassion Focused Therapy (CFT), Point 16 outlines the detailed aspects of compassion in the CFT approach. We can make a preliminary note, however, that different models of compassion are emerging based on different theories, traditions and research (Fehr, Sprecher, & Underwood, 2009). The word "compassion" comes from the Latin word *compati*, which means "to suffer with". Probably the best-known definition is that of the Dalai Lama who defined compassion as "a *sensitivity* to the suffering of self and others, with a deep *commitment* to try to relieve it", i.e., sensitive attention-awareness *plus* motivation. In the Buddhist model true compassion arises for insight into the illusory nature of a separate self and the grasping to maintain its boundaries—from what is called an enlightened or awake mind. Kristin Neff (2003a, 2003b; see www.self-compassion.org), a pioneer in the research on self-compassion, derived her model and self-report measures from Theravada Buddhism. Her approach to self-compassion involves three main components:

1 being mindful and open to one's own suffering;
2 being kind, and non self-condemning; and
3 an awareness of sharing experiences of suffering with others rather than feeling ashamed and alone—an openness to our common humanity.

In contrast, CFT was developed with and for people who have chronic and complex mental-health problems linked to shame and self-criticism, and who often come from difficult (e.g., neglectful or abusive) backgrounds. The CFT approach to compassion borrows from many Buddhist teachings (especially the roles of sensitivity to and motivation to relieve suffering) but its roots are derived from an evolutionary, neuroscience and social psychology approach, linked to the psychology and neurophysiology of caring—both giving and receiving (Gilbert, 1989, 2000a, 2005a, 2009a). Feeling cared for, accepted and having a sense of belonging and affiliation with others is fundamental to our physiological maturation and well-being (Cozolino, 2007; Siegel, 2001, 2007). These are linked to particular types of positive affect that are associated with well-being (Depue & Morrone-Strupinsky, 2005; Mikulincer & Shaver, 2007; Panksepp, 1998), and a neuro-hormonal profile of increased endorphins and oxytocin (Carter, 1998; Panksepp, 1998). These calm, peaceful types of positive feelings can be distinguished from those psychomotor activating emotions associated with achievement, excitement and resource seeking (Depue & Morrone-Strupinsky, 2005). Feeling a positive sense of well-being, contentment and safeness, in contrast to feeling excited or achievement focused, can now be distinguished on self-report (Gilbert et al., 2008). In that study, we found that emotions of contentment and safeness were more strongly associated with lower depression, anxiety and stress, than were positive emotions of excitement or feeling energized.

So, if there are *different types* of positive emotions—and there are different brain systems underpinning these positive emotions—then it makes sense that psychotherapists could focus on how to stimulate capacities for the positive emotions associated with calming and well-being. As we will see, this involves helping clients (become motivated to) develop compassion for themselves, compassion for others and the ability to be sensitive to the compassion from others. There are compassionate (and non-compassionate) ways to engage with painful experiences, frightening feelings or traumatic memories. CFT is not about avoidance of the painful, or trying to "soothe it away", but rather is a way of engaging with the painful. In Point 29 we'll note that many clients are fearful of compassionate feelings from others, and for the self, and it is working with that fear that can constitute the major focus of the work.

A second aspect of the CFT evolutionary approach suggests that self-evaluative systems operate through the same processing systems that we use when evaluating social and interpersonal processes (Gilbert, 1989, 2000a). So, for example, as behaviourists have long noted, whether we see something sexual or fantasise about something sexual, the sexual arousal system is the same—there aren't different systems for internal and external stimuli. Similarly, self-criticism and self-compassion can operate through similar brain processes that are stimulated when other people are critical of or compassionate to us. Increasing evidence for this view has come from the study of empathy and mirror neurons (Decety & Jackson, 2004) and our own recent fMRI study on self-criticism and self-compassion (Longe et al., 2010).

Interventions

CFT is a multimodal therapy that builds on a range of cognitive-behavioural (CBT) and other therapies and interventions. Hence, it focuses on attention, reasoning and rumination, behaviour, emotions, motives and imagery. It utilizes: the therapeutic relationship (see below); Socratic dialogues, guided discovery, psycho-education (of the CFT model); structured formulations; thought, emotion, behaviour and "body" monitoring; inference chaining; functional analysis; behavioural experiments; exposure, graded tasks; compassion focused imagery; chair work; enactment of different selves; mindfulness; learning emotional tolerance, learning to understand and cope with emotional complexities and conflicts, making commitments for effort and practice, illuminating safety strategies; mentalizing; expressive (letter) writing, forgiveness, distinguishing shame-criticizing from compassionate self-correction and out-of-session work and guided practice—to name a few!

Feeling the change

CFT adds distinctive features in its compassion focus and use of compassion imagery to traditional CBT-type approaches. As with many of the recent developments in therapy, special attention is given to mindfulness in both client and therapist (Siegel, 2010). In the formulation CFT is focused on the affect-regulation model outlined in Point 6, and interventions are used to develop specific patterns of affect regulation, brain states and self-experiences that underpin change processes. This is particularly important when it comes to working with self-criticism and shame in people from harsh backgrounds. Such individuals may not have experienced much in the way of caring or affiliative behaviour from others and therefore the (soothing) emotion-regulation system is less accessible to them. These are individuals who are likely to say, "I understand the logic of [say] CBT, but I can't feel any different". To *feel* different requires the ability to access affect systems (a specific neurophysiology) that give rise to our *feelings* of reassurance and safeness. This is a well-known issue in CBT (Leahy, 2001; Stott, 2007; Wills, 2009, p. 57).

Over twenty years ago I explored why "alternative thoughts" were not "experienced" as helpful. This revealed that the emotional tone, and the way that such clients "heard" alternative thoughts in their head, was often analytical, cold, detached or even aggressive. Alternative thoughts to feeling a failure, like: "Come on, the evidence does not support this negative view; remember how much you achieved last week!" will have a very different impact if said to oneself (experienced) aggressively and with irritation than if said slowly and with kindness and warmth. It was the same with exposures or home-works— the way they are done (bullying and forcing oneself verses encouraging and being kind to oneself) can be as important as what is done. So, it seemed clear that we needed to focus far more on the *feelings* of alternatives not just the content— indeed, an over focus on content often was not helpful. So, my first steps into CFT simply tried to encourage clients to imagine a warm, kind voice offering them the alternatives; or working with them in their behavioural tasks. By the time of the second edition of *Counselling for Depression* (Gilbert, 2000b) a whole focus had become concentrated on "developing inner warmth" (see also Gilbert, 2000a). So, CFT progressed from doing CBT and emotion work *with a compassion (kindness) focus* and, then, as the evidence for the model developed and more specific exercises proved helpful, on to CFT.

The therapeutic relationship

The therapeutic relationship plays a key role in CFT (Gilbert, 2007c; Gilbert & Leahy, 2007), paying particular attention to the micro-skills of therapeutic engagement (Ivey & Ivey, 2003), issues of transference/countertransference (Miranda & Andersen, 2007), expression, amplification, inhibition and/or fear of emotion (Elliott, Watson, Goldman, & Greenberg, 2003; Leahy, 2001), shame (Gilbert, 2007c), validation (Leahy, 2005), and mindfulness of the therapist (Siegel, 2010). When training people from other approaches, particularly CBT, we find that we have to slow them down; to allow spaces, and silences for reflection, and experiencing within the therapy rather than a series of

Socratic questions or "target setting". We teach how to use one's voice speed and tone, nonverbal communication, the pacing of the therapy, being mindful (Katzow & Safran, 2007; Siegel, 2010) and the reflective process in the service of creating "safeness" to explore, discover, experiment and develop. Key is to provide emotional contexts where the client can experience (and internalize) therapists as "compassionately alongside them"—no easy task because as we will discuss below (see Point 10) shame often involves clients having emotional experiences (transference) of being misunderstood, getting things wrong, trying to work out what the other person wants them to do *and intense aloneness*. The emotional tone in the therapy is created partly by the whole manner and pacing of the therapist and is important in this process of *experiencing* "togetherness". CF therapists are sensitive to how clients can actually find it hard to experience "togetherness" or "being cared about", and wrap themselves in safety strategies of sealing the self off from "the *feelings* of togetherness and connectedness" (see Point 29; Gilbert, 1997, 2007a, especially Chapters 5 and 6, 2007c).

CBT focuses on collaboration, where the therapist and client focus on the problem together—as a team. CFT also focuses on (mind) "sharing". The evolution of sharing (and motives to share), e.g., not only objects but also our thoughts, ideas and feelings, is one of humans' most important adaptations and we excel at wanting to share. As an especially social species, humans have an innate desire to share—not only material things but also their knowledge, values and the content of their minds—to be known, understood and validated. Thus, issues of motivation to share versus fear of sharing (shame), empathy and theory of mind are important evolved motives and competencies. It is the felt barriers to this "flow of minds" that can be problematic for some people and the way that the therapist "unblocks" this flow that can be therapeutic.

Dialectical Behaviour Therapy (DBT; Linehan, 1993) addresses the key issue of therapy-interfering behaviours. CFT, like any other therapy, needs to be able to set clear boundaries, and use authority as a containing process. Some clients can be "emotional bullies", threatening the therapist (e.g., with litigation or suicide) and are demanding. Frightened therapists may submit or back off. The client, at some level, is frightened of their own capacity to force others away from them. For other clients, during painful moments, therapists might try to rescue rather than be silent. So, clarification of the therapeutic relationship is very important. This is why DBT wisely recommends a support group for therapists working with these kinds of clients.

Research has shown that compassion can become a genuine part of self-identity but it can also be linked to self-image goals where people are compassionate in order to be liked (Crocker & Canevello, 2008). Compassion focused self-image goals are problematic in many ways. Researchers are also beginning to explore attachment style and therapeutic relationships with evidence that securely attached therapists develop therapeutic alliances easier and with less problems than therapists with an insecure attachment style (Black, Hardy, Turpin, & Parry, 2005; see also Liotti, 2007). Leahy (2007) has also outlined how the personality and schema organization of the therapist can play a huge role in the therapeutic relationship—for example, autocratic therapists with dependent patients, or dependent therapists with autocratic patients. So, compassion is not about submissive "niceness"—it can be tough, setting boundaries, being honest and not giving clients what they want but what they need. An alcoholic wants another drink—that is not what they need; many people want to avoid pain and may try to do so in a variety of ways—but (kind) clarity, exposure and acceptance may be what actually facilitates change and growth (Siegel, 2010).

Evidence for the benefits of compassion

Although CFT is rooted in an evolutionary, neuro- and psychological science model, it is important to recognize its heavy borrowing from Buddhist influences. For over 2500 years Buddhism has focused on compassion and mindfulness as central to enlightenment and "healing our mind". While Theravada Buddhism focuses on mindfulness and loving-(friendly)-kindness, Mahayana practices are specifically compassion focused (Leighton, 2003; Vessantara, 1993). At the end of his life the Buddha said that his main teachings were mindfulness and compassion—to do no harm to self or others. The Buddha outlined an eight-fold path for practice and training one's mind to avoid harming and promote compassion. This includes: compassionate meditations and imagery, compassionate behaviour, compassionate thinking, compassionate attention, compassionate feeling, compassion speech and compassionate livelihood. It is these multimodal components that lead to a compassionate mind. We now know that the practice of various aspects of compassion increases well-being and affects brain functioning, especially in areas of emotional regulation (Begley, 2007; Davidson et al., 2003).

The last 10 years have seen a major upsurge in exploring the benefits of cultivating compassion (Fehr et al., 2009). In an early study Rein, Atkinson and McCraty (1995) found that directing people in compassion imagery had positive effects on an indictor of immune functioning (S-IgA) while anger imagery had negative effects. Practices of imagining compassion for others, produce changes in the frontal cortex, immune system and well-being (Lutz, Brefczynski-Lewis, Johnstone, & Davidson, 2008). Hutcherson, Seppala and Gross (2008) found that a brief loving-kindness meditation increased feelings of social connectedness and affiliation towards strangers. Fredrickson, Cohn, Coffey, Pek and Finkel (2008) allocated 67 Compuware employees to a loving-kindness meditation group and 72 to waiting-list control. They found that six 60-minute weekly group sessions with home practice based on a CD of loving kindness meditations (compassion directed to self, then others, then strangers) increased positive emotions, mindfulness, feelings of purpose in life and social support, and decreased illness symptoms. Pace, Negi and Adame (2008) found that compassion meditation (for six weeks) improved immune function and neuroendocrine and behavioural responses to stress. Rockliff, Gilbert, McEwan, Lightman and Glover (2008) found that compassionate imagery increased heart rate variability and reduced cortisol in low self-critics, but not in high self-critics. In our recent fMRI study we found that self-criticism and self-reassurance to imagined threatening events (e.g., a job rejection) stimulated different brain areas, with self-compassion but not self-criticism stimulating the insula—a brain area associated with empathy (Longe et al., 2010). Viewing sad faces, neutrally or with a compassionate attitude, influences neurophysiological responses to faces (Ji-Woong et al., 2009).

In a small uncontrolled study of people with chronic mental-health problems, compassion training significantly reduced shame, self-criticism, depression and anxiety (Gilbert & Procter, 2006). Compassion training has also been found to be helpful for psychotic voice hearers (Mayhew & Gilbert, 2008). In a study of group-based CFT for 19 clients in a high-security psychiatric setting, Laithwaite et al. (2009) found ". . . a large magnitude of change for levels of depression and self-esteem . . . . A moderate magnitude of change was found for the social comparison scale and general psychopathology, with a small magnitude of change for shame, ... These changes were maintained at 6-week follow-up" (p. 521).

In the field of relationships and well-being, there is now good evidence that caring for others, showing appreciation and gratitude, having empathic and mentalizing skills, does much to build positive relationships, which significantly influence well-being and mental and physical health (Cacioppo, Berston, Sheridan, & McClintock, 2000; Cozolino, 2007, 2008). There is increasing evidence that the kind of "self" we try to become will influence our well-being and social relationships, and compassionate rather than self-focused self-identities are associated with the better outcomes (Crocker & Canevello, 2008). Taken together there are good grounds for the further development of and research into CFT.

Neff (2003a, 2003b) has been a pioneer in studies of *self-compassion* (see pages 3–4). She has shown that self-compassion can be distinguished from self-esteem and predicts some aspects of well-being better than self-esteem (Neff & Vonk, 2009), and that self-compassion aids in coping with academic failure (Neff, Hsieh, & Dejitterat, 2005; Neely, Schallert, Mohammed, Roberts, & Chen, 2009). Compassionate letter writing to oneself, improves coping with life events and reduces depression (Leary et al., 2007). As noted, however, Neff's concepts of compassion are different from the evolutionary and attachment-rooted model outlined here and, as yet, there is no agreed definition of compassion—indeed, the word compassion can have slightly (but important) different meanings in different languages. So, here compassion will be defined as a "mind set", a basic mentality, and explored in detail in Point 16.

A personal journey

My interest in developing people's capacities for compassion and self-compassion was fuelled by a number of issues:

- First, was a long interest in evolutionary approaches to human behaviour, suffering and growth (Gilbert, 1984, 1989, 1995, 2001a, 2001b, 2005a, 2005b, 2007a, 2007b, 2009a). The idea that cognitive systems tap underlying evolved motivation and emotional mechanisms has also been central to Beck's cognitive approach (Beck, 1987, 1996; Beck, Emery, & Greenberg, 1985), with a special edition dedicated to exploring the evolutionary–cognitive interface (Gilbert, 2002, 2004).
- Second, evolutionary psychology has focused significantly on the issue of altruism and caring (Gilbert, 2005a) with increasing recognition of just how important these have been in our evolution (Bowlby, 1969; Hrdy, 2009) and now are to our physical and psychological development (Cozolino, 2007) and well-being (Cozolino, 2008; Gilbert, 2009a; Siegel, 2007).
- Third, people with chronic mental-health problems often come from backgrounds of high stress and/or low altruism and caring (Bifulco & Moran, 1998), backgrounds that significantly affect physical and psychological development (Cozolino, 2007; Gerhardt, 2004; Teicher, 2002).
- Fourth, partly as a consequence of these life experiences, people with chronic and complex problems can be especially, deeply troubled by shame and self-criticism and/or self-hatred and find it enormously difficult to be open to

the kindness of others or to be kind to themselves (Gilbert, 1992, 2000a, 2007a, 2007c; Gilbert & Procter, 2006).

- Fifth, as noted on page 6, when using CBT they would typically say, "I can see the logic of alternative thoughts but I still feel X, or Y. I can understand why I wasn't to blame for my abuse but I still *feel* I'm to blame", or, "I still *feel* there is something bad about me".

- Sixth, there is increasing awareness that *the way* clients are able to think about and reflect on the contents of their own minds (e.g., competencies to mentalize in contrast to being alexithymic) has major implications for the process and focus of therapy (Bateman & Fonagy, 2006; Choi-Kain & Gunderson, 2008; Liotti & Gilbert, in press; Liotti & Prunetti, 2010).

- Last, but not least, is a long personal interest in the philosophies and practices of Buddhism—although I do not regard myself as a Buddhist as such. Compassion practices, such as becoming the compassionate self (see Part 2), may create a sense of safeness that aides the development of mindfulness and mentalizing. In Buddhist psychology compassion "transforms" the mind.

Logic and emotion

It has been known for a long time that logic and emotion can be in conflict. Indeed, since the 1980s research has shown that we have quite different processing systems in our minds. One is linked to what is called *implicit (automatic) processing*, which is non-conscious, fast, emotional, requires little effort, is subject to classical conditioning and self-identify functions, and may generate feelings and fantasies even against conscious desires. This is the system which gives that "felt sense of something". This can be contrasted with an *explicit (controlled) processing* system, which is slower, consciously focused, reflective, verbal and effortful (Haidt, 2001; Hassin, Uleman, & Bargh, 2005).

These findings have been usefully formulated for clinical work (e.g., Power & Dalgleish, 1997) with more complex models being offered by Teasdale and Barnard (1993). But the basic point is that there is no simple connection of cognition to emotion, and there are different neurophysiological systems underpinning them (Panksepp, 1998). So, one of the problems linking thinking and feeling ("I know it but I don't feel it") can be attributed to (different) implicit and explicit systems coming up with different processing strategies and conclusions. Cognitive, and many other, therapists and psychologists have not helped matters by using the concept of cognition and information processing interchangeably as if they are the same thing. They are not. Your computer and DNA—indeed every cell in your body—are information processing mechanisms but I don't think that they have "cognitions". This failure to define what is and is not "a cognition" or "cognitive" in contrast to a motive or an emotion has caused difficulties in this area of research.

Various solutions have been offered to work with the problems of feelings not following cognitions or logical reasoning, such as: needing more time to practise; most change is slow and hard work; more exposure to problematic emotions; identifying "roadblocks" and their functions (Leahy, 2001); a need for a particular therapeutic relationship (Wallin, 2007); or developing mindfulness and acceptance (Hayes, Follette, & Linehan, 2004; Liotti & Prunetti, 2010). CFT offers an additional position. CFT suggests that there can be a *fundamental problem in an implicit emotional system* that evolved with mammalian and human caring systems and which gives rise to feelings of reassurance, safeness and connectedness (see Point 6). The inability to access that affect system is what underpins this problem. Indeed, as noted (page 6), some people can cognitively (logically) generate "alternative thoughts" but hear them in their head as cold, detached or aggressive. There is no warmth or encouragement in their alternative thoughts—the emotional tone is more like cold instruction. I have found that the idea of *feeling* (inner) kindness and supportiveness as part of generating

15

alternative "thoughts" is an anathema to them. So, they just cannot "feel" their alternative thoughts and images.

These clients also have a deep-seated sense of "being to blame for their problems"; it is "their fault"; there is something "fundamentally flawed or damaged" about them—which blocks feelings of compassion and self-acceptance. It becomes clear, then, that we need to "warm up" people's ability to stand back from their thoughts, feelings and problems and treat themselves with more compassion and kindness, as well as using insight, logic, problem solving exposures and "mind training".

Case example

Over twenty years ago I worked with Jane, who suffered from a particularly chronic bipolar depression with border-line features and suicidality. She had been adopted early in childhood and had a long-lived feeling of not fitting in anywhere. She became good at generating very reasonable alternative thoughts to the idea that she was a failure and not really wanted—yet this did not shift her mood much. When I asked about the emotional tone of her alternative thoughts, whether she experienced them as reassuring, helpful and kind, she was puzzled, "Of course not," she said, "I just need to be logical. Why would I want to be kind to myself? Being kind to myself seems like a weakness and a self-indulgence! I just need to get a grip on these thoughts." Now, she was married with children and had a supportive family, so I pondered on this, "But isn't the whole point of exploring these alternative thoughts and ideas—to help you *feel* loved and wanted—to feel that support, belonging, kindness and acceptance that you seek?" I put that to her. From distant recall she said, "Yes but I don't want to be compassionate to myself—there is just too much I don't like about me!" It took some time before she recognized that she was: (1) actually closed (and dismissive) to the kindness of others because of her own self-dislike; (2) which undermined her abilities to be assertive; which then (3) led on to sub-missive resentment and feelings of powerlessness; and (4) her secret inner resenting and hating led to further feelings of self-dislike.

So, with Jane we pondered how she might generate more emotional warmth, "acceptance" and "kindness in her alternative thoughts"; the idea being that when she thought of and (maybe) wrote down alternative thoughts (to her depressing ones), she might focus on the *feelings* of warmth and reassurance in them. This was to reveal another key aspect of working with compassion—at first Jane was con-temptuous and frightened of developing warmth for herself. She was also fearful of allowing herself to *really pay attention*, and feel care from others; fearful of intense emotional closeness; that others getting close would sooner or later end in shame and rejection. Typical are beliefs of "if you *really* got close and *really* knew what goes on inside me you would not like me; you'd find out something that would turn you against me (e.g., my hateful thoughts)" or fear of dependency, e.g., "if I get close to someone then I will need them, become dependent, needy, weak and vulnerable". So, exposure to a type of *positive* (kind and affiliative) affect, and working with the *fear of feeling* this positive affect, was to prove helpful for her. Jane was one of the first to use "imagining an ideal compassionate image" (see Point 26), which she saw as a Buddha dressed as an earth Goddess! It was very tough going but she has not had a major depression relapse in over fifteen years now. Working with Jane opened up the idea that *some people are very fearful of positive emotions because of their close association with negative emotions and outcomes—and so desensitizing to, and activating of, positive and affiliative emotions requires as much work in terms of desensitization as threat-based emotions* (see Point 29).

So, at its simplest, it seems to me that people with high shame and self-criticism have difficulty in accessing feelings of (self) warmth, compassion and reassurance. This key affect-regulation system seems "off-line". As an analogy, you can have all the sexual cues, thoughts and fantasies you like but if the system in the pituitary that flushes the body with hormones is not working, these cues and fantasies will not have any physiological impact—so will not be "felt". Thus, CFT was originally developed for, and with, people who suffer from high levels of shame and self-criticism, and who find it difficult to self-sooth or generate feelings of inner warmth and self-reassurance (Gilbert, 2000a, 2000b, 2007a; Gilbert & Irons, 2005).

CFT is process rather than disorder focused because shame and self-criticism are transdiagnostic processes that have been linked to a range of psychological disorders (Gilbert & Irons, 2005; Zuroff, Santor, & Mongrain, 2005). CFT is a de-pathologizing approach that focuses more on people's (phenotypic variations in) adaptive responses to difficult environments. For example, we all have an attachment system but whether we develop the phenotypes of trusting, openness and affiliativeness or mistrust, avoidance and exploitation of others, depends upon whether we have experiences of love and care in our early life, or of neglect, hostility and abuse, and our current social contexts. The phenotype for affiliative behaviour takes on different patterns according to the context in which it develops.

The evolved mind and Compassion Focused Therapy

The Buddha and early Greek philosophers understood well that our minds are chaotic, subject to conflicts and being taken over by powerful emotions, which can throw us into problems of anxiety, depression, paranoia and violence. What they could not know is why. The beginnings of an answer came with the publication in 1859 of Darwin's *Origin of Species*, which revealed that our minds and brains are the result of natural selection. Slow changes occur as species adapt to changing environments; environments are therefore challenges that favour some individual variations within a population over others. Importantly, evolution cannot go back to the drawing board but rather builds on previous designs. This is why all animals have the same basic blueprint of four limbs, a cardio-vascular system, a digestive system, sense organs, etc. Brains, too, have basic functions, which are shared across species. This has huge implications for understanding how our minds are designed and came to be the way they are (Buss, 2003, 2009; Gilbert, 1989, 2002, 2009a; Panksepp, 1998).

Darwin's profound insights had a major impact on psychology and psychotherapy (Ellenberger, 1970). Sigmund Freud (1856–1939), for example, recognized that the mind contains many basic instincts and motives (e.g., for sex, aggression and power), which need to be regulated (lest we all just act out our desires) in a whole host of ways. So, we have various ways of keeping our lusts, passions and destructive urges under control—such as with defence mechanisms like denial, projection, dissociation and sublimation. Freud made a distinction between primary (id thinking generated by innate desires) and secondary (ego-based and reality-based) thinking. In his model the mind is inherently in conflict between desires and control. For Freud these conflicts could be overwhelming to ego consciousness and so become unconscious and a source of mental disorder. The role of the therapist was to make conscious these conflicts and help the person work through them.

Today there is much evidence that the brain does, indeed, have different systems that are linked to our passions and motives (e.g., implicit vs. explicit; Quirin, Kazen, & Kuhl, 2009) located in old brain systems such as the limbic system (MacLean, 1985), and to the regulation of motives and emotions—primarily through the frontal cortex (Panksepp, 1998). Damage these areas of the brain and impulsiveness and aggressiveness are often the major symptoms. Numerous studies using subliminal processing have shown that unconscious processing can have a major impact on emotions and behaviours (e.g., Baldwin, 2005)—in fact, consciousness is quite a late stage in information processing (Hassin et al., 2005). We also know that the mind is riddled with conflicting motives and emotions (see Point 4). Today there is also scientific study on the nature of defence mechanisms such as repression, projection and dissociation and how these affect psychological functioning, self-constructions, social relating and therapy (Miranda & Andersen, 2007).

Archetypes, motives and meanings

Few now accept the tabula rasa view of human psychology. Rather, it is recognized that the human infant comes into the world prepared to become a viable representative of its species (Knox, 2003; Schore, 1994). If all goes well the child will form attachments to his/her care givers, acquire language, develop cognitive competencies, form peer and sexual relationships and so forth. In other words, there are innate aspects to our motives and meaning making. This is not a new idea as its origins can be traced back to Plato and Kant. A person closely associated with attempts to illuminate the innate nature of the human capacity to *create different types of meaning* in psychotherapy was Jung (1875–1961).

Jung called our innate guiding systems (e.g., to seek and form early attachments to parents/carers, to belong to groups, to seek status, to discern and seek out sexual partners) *archetypes*. Archetypes influence the unfolding of development (e.g., to seek care, to become a member of a group, to find a sexual partner and become a parent, and to come to terms with death; Stevens, 1999). So, Jung postulated that humans, as an evolved species, inherit specific predispositions for thought, feeling and action. These predispositions exist as foci within the collective unconscious and serve to guide behaviour, thoughts and emotions.

Jung noted that we can see these themes of: parent–child caring, family and group loyalties and betrayal, seeking romance and love, seeking status and social position in heroic endeavour, self-sacrifice and so on—in all of the cultures, literatures and stories stretching back thousands of years. These are themes that will play out time and again in mental-health difficulties, because they are part of us—they are archetypal.

Jung also suggested that the way an archetype matures, functions and blends with other archetypes is affected by both our personality (genes) and our experience. For example, although we have an archetype that inspires and guides us towards love and comfort in the arms of our mothers when we are infants, if this relationship does not work well we can have a stunted mother archetype. Stevens (1999) refers to this as *thwarted archetypal intent*. In this case, as adults, we might spend a lot of our lives searching for a mother or father figure—trying to find someone who will love and protect us like a parent, or we can close down our need for care and love completely and shun close caring. Researchers studying these early relationships and what is called "attachment behaviour" have found that children (and adults) can indeed behave in such ways: While some are open to love and care, others are anxious about losing love and need much and constant reassurance, while yet others avoid close relationships because they are frightened, or are contemptuous and dismissive of closeness (Mikulincer & Shaver, 2007).

Jung also suggested that because our inner archetypes are designed to do different things and pursue different goals *they can be in conflict with each other* and this often causes mental-health difficulties. For Jung it is the way that these archetypal processes mature, develop and become integrated, are thwarted, or are in conflict within the self, that is the source of mental-health problems.

Social mentalities

Gilbert (1989, 1995, 2005b, 2009a) combined archetype theory with modern evolutionary, social and developmental psychology and suggested that humans have a number of "social mentalities" that enabled them to seek out and form certain types of relationship (e.g., sexual, tribal, dominant–subordinate, caring of–cared for). The basic idea is that to pursue "species general, evolved biosocial goals and motives"—such as seeking out sexual partners and forming sexual bonds, looking after one's offspring, forming friendships and alliances, developing a sense of group belonging, operating as a group member, and competing for status—brain patterns are organized in different and particular ways. A social mentality can be defined as "the organization of various psychological competencies and modules (e.g., for attention, ways of thinking, and action tendencies) *guided by motives* to secure specific types of social relationship". For example, when we are in care-*giving* mentalities we focus our attention on the distress or needs of the other, feel concern for them, work out how to provide them with what they need, engage in behaviours to do so, and feel rewarded by their recovery or prosperity. In humans this may even become linked to self-identity, e.g., "I would like to be a caring person". In a care-*seeking* mentality we are seeking inputs *from* others that will relieve distress or help us grow and develop. We turn our attention to those who are potentially helpful, signal our needs or distress and orientate our behaviours to approach others who seem to be able to offer what we think we need. We feel good if those inputs are achieved, but may feel angry, anxious or depressed if we can't find the caring inputs sought. We might then feel that others are deficient in what we need or are withholding.

In contrast, if we are competing with others we socially compare ourselves with them on relative strengths and weaknesses. We make decisions to try harder or give up. We might increase aggressive feelings or actions towards them and *turn off* concerns and feelings for any distress they might have. In this mentality our thoughts about ourselves are in terms of inferior–superior or winner–loser. If we win we might feel a buzz of good feelings, but be mildly depressed if we lose or feel inferior or defeated (Gilbert, 1984, 1992, 2007a). Linked to a self-identity, a social rank mentality can become a need to achieve (more than others), with status recognition, or a depressive sense of being a subordinate and lacking in certain qualities. There are, however, different types of achievement motivation (see Point 14). Seeing others prosper might actually make us feel envious and annoyed or bad, while seeing them fail or drop behind makes us feel good—which is, of course, quite different to being in a caring mentality!

In contrast again, when we are in co-operative alliance-building mentality our attention is focused on seeking and linking with people who are like us, who will co-operate and support us and/or pursue joint goals (playing in an orchestra, working on a team). This is linked to the evolution of our intense desires to share. We feel good when getting along with others but bad if rejected, marginalized or we feel people are cheating in some way. "Getting along" versus "getting ahead" has long been recognized to involve very different psychologies (Wolfe, Lennox, & Cutler, 1986). Lanzetta and Englis (1989) showed that priming people for co-operative or competitive relationships produced major differences in skin conductance,

23

heart rate and EMG; with co-operation promoting empathy but competitiveness "counter-empathy". So, different social mentalities can organize a whole suite of psychological and physiological processes in different ways, turning some aspects (e.g., care, sympathy or aggression) on but others off.

A simple comparison diagram for competing versus caring mentalities is offered in Figure 1.

So, according to the CFT approach our minds are organized and motivated for different goal pursuits and to create different mentalities according to the biosocial goal(s) being pursued. Clearly, mentalities overlap, some are more conscious than others, some are compensations (e.g., competing for status could be because we want affection; see Point 14), and people switch between them. Indeed, the ability to switch between them is a mark of health (Gilbert, 1989), e.g., such as the man who can compete in the job market but be a loving father at home, rather than also trying to compete with his children for his wife's affection and time. Individuals who get trapped in a particular mentality, for example, who are competitive or submissive all the time and really struggle with being co-operative or care giving or care receiving, can be disadvantaged in many ways. Paranoid patients, for example, find care receiving extremely threatening because of basic mistrust. Psychopaths find care giving and having empathic concern very difficult, but might mentalize very well in a competitive situation. So, the argument is that we have evolved brains that pursue certain social strategies, roles and relationships, and in order to pursue them different aspects of our minds are turned on and off. If we are in a (say) tribal mentality and see the other group as enemies, empathic concern and care giving (for the suffering we cause them) is firmly turned off, enabling us to behave aggressively without concern or guilt for the harm we do. There is much in psychotherapy of complex cases where we're trying to tone down some mentalities and activate others. Beck, Freeman and Davis (2003) took a somewhat similar evolutionary view in their approach to personality disorders.

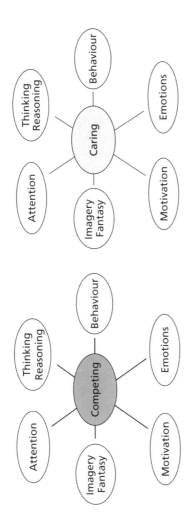

Figure 1 A comparison of competitive and caring mentalities

The way that social mentalities develop, mature, blend and are activated is linked to genes, background and current social demands. This is important because CFT takes an *interactional and compensatory* view of the way the mind is organized. For example, children who are abused or neglected learn that care eliciting, turning to others for help and being soothed by them is unlikely to happen, is unhelpful or even threatening/dangerous. Rather, the need to pay attention to the power and potential for being harmed/shamed by others is needed. This will shift their development into a threat-focused, social rank mentality (competitive system), which will orientate them to be very attentive to cues of aggressiveness/rejection. Liotti (2000, 2002, 2007) outlined how children can become disorganized in their attachment behaviour especially when the care giver becomes the source of both safety and threat. In such cases children can become disorganized in their social mentality coherence, switching between submissiveness, aggressiveness withdrawal and closeness seeking in ways that are difficult for them or others around them to understand.

CFT also takes an interactional view to the extent that work on one social mentality, such as care eliciting or care providing (through compassion), can have profound effects on the organization of other social mentalities (Gilbert, 1989). Again, this is not a new view. Buddhism has long argued that compassion transforms and reorganizes the mind; and Jung argued that the process of individuation was a process of organizing and reorganizing our archetypal potentials.

The bottom line is that we need to understand that the brain is an evolved organ that is *designed to function in certain ways* and change its patterns in different contexts and goal pursuits. It seeks out certain inputs (e.g., affiliative relations with other minds), responds to those inputs, and shows defensive, developmental deviations if those inputs are not forthcoming. Some psychotherapies and most psychiatric classifications do not address this and are content to rely on how things look from the outside. CFT sits within the tradition of understanding our minds in terms of their evolved design and particularly our human biosocial goals and *needs*, e.g., for affection, care, protection, belonging; and human competencies such as mentalizing, theory of mind, empathy, capabilities for fantasy and imagination, as we now explore.

Multi-mind

We know that different psychologies (motives, emotions and cognitive competencies) have been laid down at different times in evolution. For example, capacities for sex, fighting, hunting and gaining and defending a territory can be traced back to the reptiles over 500 million years ago and before them. It was not until the evolution of the mammals (about 120 million years ago) that psychologies (supported by emotions and motivational systems) for infant-caring, alliance formation, play, and status hierarchies came into the world. It was not until about 2 million years ago that the competencies for complex thinking, reflection, theory of mind and having a sense of self and self-identity, began to emerge. So, brains have evolved in a series of stages, making our minds full of a variety of different motives and emotions originating at different times, many of which can conflict.

Old and new brain

One way to think about this, and to talk to clients about it, is that we have an old brain that has various emotions and motivations that we share with many other animals, but that we also have the abilities of thinking, reflecting, observing, and forming a self-identity (Gilbert, 2009a). Problems can arise in the way our old brain and new brain interact. For example, bodily sensations when linked to the new brain abilities that can think, reason and give explanations may conclude that "my increased heart rate means I am going to have a heart attack and die", which fosters panic attacks. Our reflection that "this mistake means I am a failure, unlovable with no future", can accentuate depression. Animals don't get stressed out by worrying about paying the mortgage, what the future might hold, what will happen to the children if they don't study hard, whether this lump or pain means an oncoming cancer—these are all created because of our ability to think in certain "meta" ways (Wells, 2000).

A variety of mental states

The fact that we have many different motives, archetypal potentials and the like, that have evolved over many millions of years, and these different potentials can give rise to serious problems, is well known now, even noted in most introductory psychology undergraduate textbooks. For example, Coon (1992) opened his introductory undergraduate text on psychology with this graphic depiction:

> You are a universe, a collection of worlds within worlds. Your brain is possibly the most complicated and amazing device in existence. Through its action you are capable of music, art, science, and war. Your potential for love and compassion coexists with your potential for aggression, hatred . . . Murder?
>
> (p. 1)

What Coon and other researchers suggest is that *we are not unified selves*, despite our experience of being so. Rather, we are made up of many different possibilities for the creation of meaning and generating brain patterns and states of mind. As Ornstein (1986) put it over twenty years ago:

> The long progression in our self-understanding has been from a simple and usually "intellectual" view to the view that the mind is a mixed structure, for it contains a complex set of "talents", "modules" and "policies" within. . . . All

these general components of the mind can act independently of each other; they may well have different priorities.

The discovery of increased complexity and differentiation has occurred in many different areas of research, . . . in the study of brain functions and localization; in the conceptions of the nature of intelligence; in personality testing; and in theories of the general characteristics of the mind.

(p. 9)

In fact, the idea of there being complex subsystems and programmes in our mind, and how they interact, has been a focus of theorizing in CBT. For example, Beck (1996) posited the existence of a variety of different "modes", where each mode represented integrated motivational, emotional and cognitive systems—a view that has some similarity to archetype and social mentality ideas. In the same tradition Teasdale and Barnard (1993) posited a range of cognitive, emotional and motivational processing subsystems that interact.

In some ways both Coon and Ornstein are offering a modern exposition of the archetypal nature of the human mind, and they echo another Jungian idea—that although we often think of ourselves as somehow whole and integrated individuals this is an illusion. In fact, Jung suggested that integration and wholeness are psychological feats—maturational accomplishments. We are made up of many different talents, abilities, social motives, emotions, and so on, and coping with their various pushes and pulls is no easy matter.

This mixed bag of motives and meaning-creating modules (archetypes) can give rise to the experience of not one self but a variety of selves (e.g., Rowan, 1990). These possible selves or subpersonalities can feel different things and play different parts when we are in different states of mind. In therapy we can even learn to name these different selves and speak with them. We can recognize the bullying self, the perfectionist self, the vengeful-sadist self, the sexual self, the forgiving self, and so on. Another way to think of this is as the potential to enact

31

different social roles requiring different social mentalities (and brain patterns; Gilbert, 1989, 1992; Gilbert & Irons, 2005; Gilbert & McGuire, 1998).

Mentalizing and the sense of self

CBT was originally developed for those who are aware of their thoughts and emotions, and can articulate them fairly easily—as captured by various assessment scales (e.g., Safran & Segal, 1990). Therapists then use this skill to direct clients' attention to their styles of thinking or core beliefs and schema. However, we now know that the *competencies* that underpin our capacities to become aware of our motives, emotions and thoughts, and our ability to articulate, think about and reflect on them, are very complex and follow a developmental process. Evolutionists have long pointed out that some motivational processes may be almost impossible to bring to consciousness. These are complex facets of our multi-minds.

Over the last 10 years there has been accelerated interest *in the way* that humans link self-understanding and self-identity to attending and reasoning about internal emotions and thoughts. We know, for example, that the brain is capable of generating a huge array of competing and complex emotions and (and at times bizarre and unpleasant) thoughts/fantasies, which have to be organized in a coherent fashion for individuals to have a coherent sense of self (Gilbert, 2005a; McGregor & Marigold, 2003). People can be deeply troubled and overwhelmed by some of the contents of their mind. New information (feelings, fantasies, thoughts) that threatens the sense of self and self-identity, even if it promises to produce positive change, can be actively resisted. Swann, Rentfrow and Guinn (2003) suggested that people seek coherence, familiarity and predictability in their self-identities, not just self-enhancement. Thus, submissive or aggressive self-identities can resist change (see Leary & Tangney, 2003, for a detailed discussion of these issues, and Point 29 in this volume).

One way coherence is achieved is through the ability to reflect on and understand the contents of one's own mind and those of others—and the ability to use this information to navigate in and out of different types of social role and social relationship. Mentalizing clearly aids the use and organization of our social mentalities (Allen, Fonagy, & Bateman, 2008). This takes us to the heart of how our newly evolved brains, which give rise to types of reasoning and competencies to generate a self-identity, interact with old brain emotions and motives—those basic strategies for survival and reproduction that have evolved over a very long time (Gilbert, 1989, 2009a).

Unfortunately (as with so much in psychotherapy research and therapy) one of the problems with this area of study (the competencies underpinning capacities for reflection on mental states) is that it is riddled with different approaches, concepts and theories, many of which significantly overlap and research is yet to clarify. For example, being able to pay attention to, think about, reflect on and contain different feelings, along with how we attribute different causes and meanings to our and other people's mental states, has been linked to: emotional schemas, alexithymia, mentalization, theory of mind, empathy and sympathy, emotional intelligence, experiential avoidance, mindfulness, the use of projective defences and Asperger syndrome (e.g., Choi-Kain & Gunderson, 2008), to name just a few!

Taking just the one example of alexithymia—this describes difficulties in recognizing and identifying feelings at a subjective level, difficulties in describing and reflecting on feelings, especially difficulties in describing ambivalence and conflicts of feelings, and tendencies to focus on external events rather than internal ones (e.g., Meins, Harris-Waller, & Lloyd, 2008). These authors also found evidence that some of these difficulties are linked to (insecure) attachment history. There is increasing evidence that alexithymic-type difficulties are prevalent in a wide range of mental-health difficulties—especially those associated with trauma (Liotti & Prunetti, 2010). It is also likely that there are many individuals, perhaps successful in business or politics, who have alexithymic traits but do not manifest current definitions of mental-health difficulties— although their insensitivities may create them in others. We know, too, that some people simply justify their own positions, thoughts and behaviours in all kinds of ways without reflection or apparent doubt—and helping people get beyond that, by being more open, reflective and accepting of responsibility, and entering into genuine dialogue, can be difficult. Justifiers and externalizers, however, often don't attend therapy—because they see no reason to, "there's nothing wrong with them"—and may be highly shame avoidant. So, they simply act out in all kinds of non-reflective ways.

Meins et al. (2008) suggested that the alexithymic trait of externally oriented thinking can arise from a *conscious decision* not to explore the contents of one's mind (motives, thoughts and feelings) and this should be distinguished from an inability to do so. Koren-Karie, Oppenheim, Dolev, Sher and Etzion-Carasso (2002) found that while some mothers were able to think about the minds of their babies, other (disengaged) mothers found this distressing and actively avoided doing so. These mothers were likely to have insecurely attached children.

Add into this complexity processes by which we use projection and projective identification (Miranda & Andersen, 2007) to understand our own minds and those of others (including how we create our religious thoughts and fantasies; Bering, 2002) and you can see that our "new brain" can get into some right tangles with emotions and motives emerging from the old brain!

Development of psychological competencies

In CFT competencies such as empathy and mentalizing enable social mentalities to function at increasingly complex levels. Competencies mature and unfold over time. So, in addition to the aspects, such as alexithymia and mentalizing, that influence *how* we think about our states of mind, we also need to think about developmental processes—these are not static skills. CBT therapists have drawn attention to the fact that clients will have different cognitive abilities linked to Piagetian stages of cognitive development (Rosen, 1993). For example, some will be much more preoperational (difficulties in thinking in abstract terms and reflecting on inner states) than others. So, people's abilities to reflect on their inner feelings and those of others is clearly linked to these cognitive abilities (see also Kegan, 1982, for an important discussion). We also know that people's *theory of mind* competencies develop over time—and may be linked to other cognitive abilities. We further know that people's abilities to think and reason morally develop over time moving from simple concepts of right and wrong, according to what adults punish or reward, to much more abstract thinking but are also influenced by social context (Gilbert, 1989).

Piaget also drew a distinction between assimilation (how new information is made to fit with current beliefs) and accommodation (new information causes an internal change and transformation in knowledge organization and insight). Another aspect here is "openness" to new possibilities and to change, which in turn butts up against concepts of motivation and "readiness to change".

Another related area of importance to CFT is that of emotional maturation. For example, Lane and Schwartz (1987) suggested that affect complexity relates to the ability to differentiate different emotions and experience. They suggest a set of stages that may parallel Piaget's cognitive stages. These are awareness of:

1 bodily sensations;
2 the body in action;
3 individual feelings;
4 blends of feelings; and
5 blends of blends of feelings.

At the lowest level, the baby is only aware of experiences in body sensations and these are generally crudely differentiated in some pleasure–pain dimension. Subsequently comes the awareness of feelings derived from actions. Later comes the more differentiated affects of sadness, anger, anxiety, joy, etc. Later comes the capacity to experience blends of these feelings and the capacity to cope with ambivalence. Later still comes blends of blends of feelings. The way this emotional maturation takes place is still not well understood but we know that the mentalizing abilities of the parent, and their affection, are crucial. Clients who struggle with understanding their emotions and get stuck at lower levels of emotional awareness are certainly going to struggle with compassion and it's not surprising that many of them will not be able to understand what compassion feels like—because *emotions in general* are problematic to them (see Point 29).

Increasingly, therapists are realizing that part of their role (not only with the more severe mental-health problems) is to advance the patient's capacity for mindfulness and mentalizing, to be less avoidant, judgemental and self-critical, becoming able to reflect on their feelings, to better understand blends of feelings, conflicts between feelings, conditioned emotions (and emotional memories) and positive and negative beliefs about feelings (see also Gilbert, 1992, Chapter 4). The benefits of this is that clients become tolerant and more accepting of their feelings, rather than fighting or avoiding them, and more open to relationships based on genuine efforts to understand the mind of others.

Social mentalities and mentalizing

The link between these kinds of awareness and competencies like mentalizing—and those linked to the pursuit of social roles, social mentalities and self-identity, is complex. Recently, Liotti and Prunetti (2010) suggested that the way we mentalize is linked into social mentalities. For example, individuals who feel safe in a particular role, such as talking co-operatively with their therapist, may be able to mentalize reasonably well; but if their care-eliciting mentality is activated (and thus their attachment systems) this may be very threatening to the client and over-whelm their ability to mentalize. Liotti (December 2009, per-sonal communication) suggests that we shouldn't see mentalizing as an all-or-nothing phenomenon but rather depen-dent on a number of other conditions—especially the degree of safeness that individuals feel. Threat activation can turn off mentalizing because mentalizing is a high-level functioning competency but threat activation is designed to select from a menu of attentional and response systems for rapid action (Liotti & Gilbert, in press). Since some mentalities and motives or needs are more threatening than others there can be differ-ences in mentalizing about and within each—which can catch out the therapist.

I suggest that compassion exercises can create a sense of safeness that facilitates mentalizing. This is especially true when we teach the "compassionate self" exercise because it focuses on holding the client in a soothing and soothed position (see Point 21). We are still developing the research methodology for exploring this, but indirect evidence noted above for the value of compassion (pages 9–12) suggests that this is a useful avenue of research. One can also help clients understand mentalizing by helping them slow down and recognize that there are *many different parts* to the self, with different thoughts and feelings from each (and not to identify with any specific part)—we call this multi-mind.

Obviously, I have only touched on this complex area here, but CFT therapists need to be aware of these different degrees of abilities (competencies)—clients' (developmental) abilities to think about, and reflect on, "that which arises from within one's own mind". This is going to be key to compassion work because we teach clients to take a compassionate look at the contents of their minds—in part because much of it is archetypal and was not designed by us but by evolution and personal life experiences (so is not our fault).

So, given our multi-minds, one thing is clear, we are not an integrated coherent whole self, but are rather made up of a variety of motives and competencies that combine and interact in complex ways. We have the illusion of being a single self because having a multitude of desires and possible roles and selves, not having a sense of a single self-identity, would create just *too much flexibility*, competing possibilities for thought and actions and incoherence (McGregor & Marigold, 2003). Many psychologists now see "the self" and "self-identity" as organizing processes that co-ordinate memories, emotions, beliefs and other processes to create a cohesive sense of self that allows a feeling of consistency or continuation and enables social relationships. Hence, if we require development and a reorganization of our basic mentalities (e.g., to become more assertive and competitive, recognize and process anger, or become more caring and compassionate) this can threaten self-identity and our sense of cohesion.

So, our sense of self is an organizational *feat*, and when the organization of our potentials within us breaks down (or e.g., we become overwhelmed by anxiety, rage, intrusions of trauma memories, a sense of loneliness or submissive withdrawal) we can have mental-health problems (see, e.g., Leary & Tangney, 2003, for reviews). Indeed, people talk about losing control of "parts of themselves" or "falling apart".

This turns us to the question of what enables us to cope with our multiple (helpful or destructive) potentials for thoughts, feelings and deeds, and transitions of states of mind. Also, what enables us to open up and explore new potentials within us and integrate them into our sense of self in what Jung would call an "individuation process". One answer is *compassion*, because compassion creates conditions that facilitate openness, caring, safeness and integration (Gilbert, 2005a, 2005c). Compassion from without and self-compassion from within, facilitate acceptance and tolerance, thus creating brain patterns that make exploring and integrating different elements of our mind easier.

Attachment and the importance of affection

The importance of affection

CFT is a distinctively physiology-informed therapy that is concerned with the nature, evolved functions and structure of our brains. In CFT, compassion is rooted in the evolved and socially shaped motives and mentalities that underpin altruism and care giving. Gilbert (1989, 2005a) suggested that two sources of altruism (with the motivating and processing systems) underpin compassion: One is kin altruism and attachment systems of caring, the other is based on reciprocal altruism and desires for moral and fair/just social relationships. More complex models are now developing (e.g., Hrdy, 2009).

When we take an evolutionary approach, one of the most central mammalian qualities, what stands out above those of sex, fighting and status seeking, is the huge importance of caring. We now know that the evolution of caring came with profound changes in central and peripheral nervous systems—one major adaptation being the regulation of fight and flight to enable closeness, and for physical closeness to have "soothing properties". For example, in the brain the endorphins and the hormone oxytocin evolved to regulate threat processing (inhibiting fight/flight) and promote social interest and caring (Bell, 2001; Wang, 2005). Porges (2003, 2007) detailed how the evolution of the myelinated vagus nerve (to the heart) has supported interpersonal approach behaviours that enable social affiliations, caring and sharing. The myelinated vagus nerve evolved with attachment and the ability for infants to be calmed by parental caring behaviours (Carter, 1998; Depue &

Morrone-Strupinsky, 2005). This addition to the autonomic nervous system can inhibit sympathetically driven threat-defensive behaviours (e.g., fight/flight) and hypothalamic–pituitary–adrenal (HPA) axis activity, and promote a calm physiological state, conducive to interpersonal closeness and social affiliation. In general, the safer people feel, the more open and *flexible* they can be in response to their environment (Porges, 2003, 2007). This is reflected in the dynamic balancing of the sympathetic and parasympathetic nervous systems that give rise to the variability in heart rate (HRV; Porges, 2007). Hence, feeling interpersonally safe is linked to HRV, and higher HRV is linked to a greater ability to *self*-sooth (quick to be able to tone down threat processing) when stressed (Porges, 2007).

Leaving aside the neurophysiology of caring, one of the most important evolutionary models of the last 40 years is that of the attachment theory of John Bowlby (1907–1990) (Mikulincer & Shaver, 2007); with somewhat similar concerns being taken up by acceptance–rejection theory (Rohner, 1986, 2004). (See also Hrdy, 2009, for the importance of multiple care givers in human evolution.) These profoundly important theories have stimulated considerable research into the way in which children and parents interact such that the interactions have major effects on a child's brain and psychological competencies (Cozolino, 2007; Siegel, 2001). For many mammals affection has evolved as a key to the regulation of motives and emotions. For humans there is now considerable evidence that if one feels cared for, as opposed to neglected or rejected, this has major effects on our physiological states and states of mind (Cozolino, 2007; Gerhardt, 2004; Porges, 2007). As we will see later, CFT is rooted in this evolutionary understanding of the huge significance of the evolution of affection and affiliation.

For species without attachment systems, such as turtles, their life expectancy is short. The mother may lay hundreds of eggs and only 1–2% survive to reproduce. However, with mammals, providing a safe, secure base from external threats, and being responsive to distress calls (MacLean, 1985) was central to Bowlby's attachment theory (1969, 1973, 1980), making attachment primarily *a threat-protection regulation system* (MacDonald, 1992). Bowlby (1969, 1973, 1980) was one of the first to consider the implications of evolved security providing for infants and its effects on infant development, emotional regulation and internalization of "working models of self and others" (Mikulincer & Shaver, 2007).

Multiple domains of caring

Over time, mammalian parenting has evolved, becoming increasingly elaborate, so that human parenting is now highly multi-faceted with: *protection* (keeping infants out of harm's way and coming to the rescue), *provisioning* (e.g., milk with antibodies, food, warmth, and other resources necessary for development), *soothing* (calming distress in the infant and "containing"), *stimulating emotion systems* (presenting facial expressions and play opportunities), *mediating* (the infant's exposure to the world), *teaching and socializing* (teaching about the world and social relating rules, setting boundaries), *validation* and "*mind sharing*" (emotional coaching and mentalizing; Hrdy, 2009). All these influence a range of brain-maturation processes and psychological competencies (Cozolino, 2007; Gerhadt, 2004; Gilbert, 1989, 2005a; Siegel, 2001, 2007; Wallin, 2007). Over time (in humans) there evolve potentials for other kin (e.g., siblings and aunts) to play a role in infant care. Indeed, humans seem particularly adapted to share caring, so that the infant/child interacted with many others who would care for him/her. This may have facilitated the psychological motives to seek out caring from (different) others and the psychological desires and competencies to read the (caring) intentions of others (Hrdy, 2009). In addition, throughout life humans are highly motivated to be liked, desired, valued and approved of (Barkow, 1989; see Gilbert, 1992, especially Chapter 7, 1997, 2007a, especially Chapter 5, 2007c).

We now know that affectionate caring, associated with feeling wanted and valued, has far-reaching and multiple effects on the physiological maturation of the infant (Cozolino, 2007; Hofer, 1994). For primates, and humans especially, the power of nurturing relationships, from a variety of individuals (parents, friends and lovers), to impact on physiologies throughout life, has become profound (Cacioppo et al., 2000; Cozolino, 2008; Schore, 1994). Because CFT concepts of compassion are based on these processes, the complexities of caring relationships should be kept in mind when considering compassion and CFT (see Point 16). This evolutionary and physiologically based approach, rather than (say) Buddhist, is the foundation for CFT.

Affect regulation: The three affect-regulation systems, caring and CFT

Our biosocial goals and *motivations* for (say) sex, status, attachments and achievements are guided by *emotions*. When we are successfully pursuing our biosocial goals and motivations we get a flush of positive emotions, whereas when there are obstacles and threats we experience threat-based emotions. Research in emotional processing has revealed a number of integrated circuits in the brain that give rise to different types of emotion that regulate motivation (Panksepp, 1998).

A useful, if simplified, model derived from recent research (Depue & Morrone-Strupinsky, 2005; LeDoux, 1998; Panksepp, 1998) has revealed that our brains contain at least three *types* of major emotion-regulation systems. Each one is designed to do different things. These three interacting systems are depicted in Figure 2.

Figure 2 The interaction between our three major emotion-regulation systems. First published in Gilbert, P. (2009a) *The Compassionate Mind*. London: Constable & Robinson and Oaklands, CA: New Harbinger. Reproduced with permission

1 The threat and self-protection system

The function of this system is to detect and pick up on threats quickly and select a response, e.g., fight, flight, freeze or some other coping efforts, and give us bursts of emotions such as anxiety, anger or disgust. These feelings will ripple through our bodies alerting us and urging us to take action against the threat. The system will also be activated if there are threats to people we love, our friends or our group. Although it is a source of painful and difficult feelings (e.g., anxiety, anger, disgust), keep in mind and explain to clients that it evolved as a *protection* system. In fact, our brain gives more priority to dealing with threat than to pleasurable things (Baumeister, Bratslavsky, Finkenauer, & Vohs, 2001). The threat system operates with particular brain systems, such as the amygdala and the hypothalamic–pituitary–adrenal (HPA) axis (LeDoux, 1998). When in threat mode, attention, thinking and reasoning, behaving, emotions and motives, and images and fantasies, can all be threat focused, with each aspect of our minds orientated to the goal of protection and safety. So, we can call this "threat mind" because different faculties of our mind are organized in a particular way (see Point 4). Once animals and humans are happy with their coping with a specific threat, there may be little arousal in the presence of threat cues, and it is only when those safety strategies are blocked that "threat mind" is reactivated. As we will note later, safety behaviours and strategies can reduce arousal in the short term, but may have longer-term, unintended and very unhelpful consequences (Gilbert, 1993; Salkovskis, 1996; Thwaites & Freeston, 2005).

So the threat system picks up on threats quickly (focusing and biasing attention) and then gives us bursts of feeling such as anxiety, anger or disgust. These feelings ripple through our bodies, alerting and urging us to take action to do something about the threat—to self-protect. The behavioural outputs include those of fight, flight and submission (Gilbert, 2001a, 2001b; Marks, 1987). Partly because the system is orientated for "better safe than sorry" (Gilbert, 1998) it is easily conditioned (Rosen & Schulkin, 1998). The genetic and synaptic regulation of serotonin plays a role in the functioning of the threat-protection system (Caspi & Moffitt, 2006). Problems with the threat system are linked to:

1 the type of triggers that activate the threat-protection system, which are linked to the nature of the threat, conditioned emotional responses, and personal meanings;
2 the type and forms of the threat-protection response, e.g., anger or anxiety, fight or flight, heart rate, nausea, sweating, flushing, racing thoughts and attentional focusing;
3 the rapidity and intensity of the threat-protection response;
4 the duration of the threat-protection response and the means and ways of calming aversive threat arousal;
5 the frequency of activation of the threat-protection system linked to external contextual cues (e.g., living in a violent household) and internal cues (self-criticism, rumination, worry);
6 the way different forms of coping (e.g., experiential avoidance, and unhelpful safety strategies) or the collapse in mentalizing abilities accentuate a sense of threat, thus further activating elements 1 to 5.

As pointed out elsewhere (Gilbert, 1989, 1993), nearly all psychotherapies focus to a greater or lesser degree on the complexities of threat self-protection but with different types of theories and methods for engaging with problems in this system.

We also know that threat processing and responding are complex. For example, emotional memories, including threat memories, are stored in different systems such as sensory (amygdala) and event-memory (hippocampal) systems, which can conflict; as in the case of someone who has an experience of fear in a flashback and feels as if the trauma is happening again (Brewin, 2006; Lee, 2005). Certain types of fear can interfere with the ability to mentalize (Liotti & Prunetti, 2010). We also know that different defensive emotions and action tendencies can conflict; one can't be in fight and flight at the same time—although we can feel both anxious and angry in the context of a social conflict, or we may even wish to cry (Dixon, 1998). Conflicts *between different* emotions and "what to do?" increase with stress. We can become anxious of losing control to anger, or angry at being inhibited and anxious. Stress can also be created through approach-avoidance conflicts, such as hating one's job but needing to stay there because of the money to pay a mortgage—which leads to feelings of entrapment (Gilbert, 2001a, 2001b, 2007a).

Emotional complexity

It is useful to help clients recognize that in any distressed state of mind there can be multiple feelings and conflicts. For example, Kim suffered from depression and anxiety. Following an argument with her partner she felt overwhelmed with feelings. So, we wondered if this could be because of *multiple* feelings, conflicts between feelings, and conflicts and dilemmas within the relationship.We could then draw a circle and put "feel terrible" at the centre and around it brain stormed the feelings that were part of that. They included: anger, anxiety, hopelessness, feeling alone and misunderstood, wanting to stay and wanting to leave, blaming him and blaming me, powerlessness, doubt, sadness, tearfulness, etc. It is also possible to help clients explore if they tend to focus on one type of feeling (e.g., anger) to block out and avoid (or an inability to process) other feelings (e.g., of powerlessness, or sadness–grief). It might then be possible to reflect and mentalize *on each individual element* of that distressed mind state—helping clients to do this for themselves rather than being overwhelmed with complexity and competing feelings.

So, threat processing is complex and it helps to reveal this to clients, clarifying with them how their brains work, why we go into threat states, and working out the precise difficulties in the threat system for that person.

2 The incentive and resource-seeking, drive-excitement system

The function of this system is to give us positive feelings that guide, motivate and encourage us to seek out resources that we (and those we love and care about) will need in order to survive and prosper (Depue & Morrone-Strupinsky, 2005). We are motivated and pleasured by seeking out, consuming and achieving nice things (e.g., food, sex, comforts, friendships, status and recognition). If we win a competition, pass an exam or get to go out with a desired person, we can have feelings of excitement and pleasure. If you win the lottery and become a millionaire you might feel a mild hypomania—feel so energized that it may be difficult to sleep, your mind will be racing and you may want to party all the time: the drive-excitement system gets out of balance. People with manic depression can have problems with this system because it can shift from too high to too low activation. When balanced with the other two systems, this system guides us towards important life goals. When blocks to our wants and goals become "a threat", the threat system kicks in with anxiety or frustration–anger.

This system is primarily an activating and "go getting" system. A substance in our brain called dopamine is important for our drives. People who take amphetamine or cocaine try to get "the dopamine" energized and hyped-up good feeling. The come down, however, is of course the opposite. We will refer to this as the drive-excitement system for short and to help us keep in mind its focus on *activated* positive feelings and motives. As we will see, though, some achievement-focused drive is defensive (see Point 14).

Thwarting incentives and goals

However, as pointed out some time ago, blocks and thwarting of our drives, goals and incentives, typically activates the threat system (e.g., anxiety, frustration, anger)—until we either

COMPASSION FOCUSED THERAPY

overcome the block or "disengage" from the goal (Klinger, 1977). Disengaging and giving up a goal or aspiration can underpin a dip in mood (e.g., sadness), and the greater the implications for the self and network of other goals of giving up are, the bigger the dip in mood. Some depressions are linked to continuing to pursue goals that cannot be achieved (craving for) and a failure of disengagements and realignment of (achievable) goals (Gilbert, 1984; Klinger, 1977), e.g., the person who can't come to terms with losses (e.g., of a relationship), set backs, illnesses and injuries. There is much in Klinger's incentive disengagement approach that fits well with Acceptance Commitment Therapy (Hayes et al., 2004). In CFT goal pursuits are examined for their functions—especially those linked to different forms of achievement (see Point 14).

3 The soothing, contentment and the safeness system

This system enables us to bring a certain soothing, quiescence and peacefulness to the self, which helps to restore our balance. When animals aren't defending themselves against threats and problems, and don't need to achieve or do anything (they have sufficient or enough), they can be *content* (Depue & Morrone-Strupinsky, 2005). Contentment is a form of being happy with the way things are and feeling safe; not striving or wanting; an inner peacefulness that is a quite different positive feeling from the hyped-up, excitement or "striving and succeeding" feeling of the drive-excitement systems. It is also different from just low threat, which can be associated with boredom or a kind of emptiness. When people practice meditation and "slowing down", these are the feelings they report; not-wanting or striving, feeling calmer inside and connected to others.

What complicates this system, but is of great importance for our exploration of compassion, is that it is also linked to affection and kindness. For example, when a baby or child is distressed, the love of the parent soothes and calms the infant. Affection and kindness from others helps sooth us adults too when we're distressed, and gives us feelings of safeness in our everyday lives. These feelings of soothing and safeness work through brain systems similar to those that produce peaceful feelings associated with fulfilment and contentment such as the *endorphins*. The hormone *oxytocin* is also linked to our feelings of social safeness and (along with the endorphins) gives us feelings of well-being that flow from feeling loved, wanted and safe with others (Carter, 1998; Wang, 2005). This system is a central focus in compassion training because it is vital to our sense of well-being. I will refer to it as a *soothing and contentment system*.

Depue and Morrone-Strupinsky (2005) linked the two positive affect-regulating systems to different types of social behaviour. They distinguished affiliation from agency and sociability. Agency and sociability are linked to control and achievement seeking, social dominance and the (threat-focused) avoidance of rejection and isolation. Warm and affiliative interactions, however, are linked to social connectedness and safeness as conferred by the presence and support of others. Affiliative social relationships calm participants, alter pain thresholds, the immune and digestive systems, and operate via the oxytocin–opiate system (Depue & Morrone-Strupinsky, 2005). There is increasing evidence that oxytocin is linked to social support and buffers stress; those with lower oxytocin having higher stress responsiveness (Heinrichs, Baumgartner, Kirschbaum, & Ehlert, 2003). Oxytocin also impacts on threat processing in the amygdala.

CFT makes a big distinction between safety seeking and safeness. Safety seeking is linked to the threat system and is about preventing or coping with threats. Safeness is a state of mind that enables individuals to be content and at peace with themselves and the world with relaxed attention and the ability to explore (Gilbert, 1993). Safeness in not the same as low activity—when we feel safe we can be active and energized. If some individuals try to create states of safeness by, say, isolation and keeping their distance from others then we see this as more safety seeking. The problem with this is that the brain can read isolation/disconnection itself as a threat and, in addition, this safety behaviour cuts them off from a natural regulator of threat—the endorphin–oxytocin system for affiliation. So, although avoidance and isolation may work to a degree, it's difficult to know how this action affects well-being. Certainly, research has shown that social anhedonia—the (in)ability to experience pleasure from social relationships—is linked to a range of psychological difficulties.

Evolutionary functional analysis

A number of key points arise from understanding the nature and origins of our emotions and what they are designed for; *what their functions are*. The first is that many negative emotions such as anxiety, anger, disgust and sadness are a normal part of our emotional repertoire. Like diarrhoea and vomiting, they are unpleasant but have basic protective functions, and even when having harmful effects are not necessarily pathologies (Nesse & Ellsworth, 2009). So important are our protection emotions that they are the big, emotional players in our brains and can easily override positive emotions (Baumeister et al., 2001). We can also explain to our clients that our brains did not evolve for happiness but for survival and reproduction, so sometimes we need to learn how to accept, tolerate and work with difficult emotions or low moods; these are not evidence of "something wrong" with us but can be quite normal responses to things in our life.

Second, it follows that our emotion systems may be working perfectly normally but the inputs are problematic. Someone who feels trapped in, say, a loveless relationship may become depressed, which can be accentuated by their focus, beliefs and ruminations, of course, but the depression can also partly be a *normal* consequence of this situation in which they find themselves. It is very hard to control your "stress-cortisol output" if you are being bullied. Some people's lives *are* stressful—or they may have experienced tragedies and losses and that's why they feel sad or are grieving. Of course, there are things we can do to amplify threat-based feelings by how we think (Wills, 2009; Dryden, 2009) or engage in various forms of avoidance (Hayes et al., 2004) but it is important to help people normalize and recognize that some of our unpleasant feelings and reactions are not abnormal but need to be engaged with—compassionately.

The third issue is to recognize that modern societies are, in a whole variety of ways, over stimulating both our threat (unstable employment, house repossession, poverty) and drive ("want more and need to do more") systems and playing havoc with our needs for connectedness and focus of social comparison (Gilbert, 2009a; Pani, 2000; Wilkinson & Pickett, 2009). Twenge, Gentile, DeWall, Ma, Lacefield and Schurtz (2010) produced a major review of evidence that mental health difficulties have been increasing at an alarming rate, especially in younger people. They attribute much of the cause for this to cultural shifts towards extrinsic goals such as individualism and materialism with competitive and rank-focused self-evaluation, and away from intrinsic goals such as cooperation, community and sharing. So, we need to socially contextualize shame and mental-health issues.

Affiliation, warmth and affection

We have seen that the evolution of attachment is one of the most fundamental aspects of the mammalian mind. Also, the evolution of attachment had a major impact on the evolution of emotional-regulation systems and in particular the importance of a social soothing system that operates with endorphins and oxytocin. This system and these neuro-hormones play a special role in regulating threat and threat arousal.

However, different types of caring will impact and stimulate the soothing system in different ways. For example, caring can be with or without warmth and affection (MacDonald, 1992) but it is warmth that is probably most associated with soothing and endorphin release (Wang, 2005). Warmth involves a number of qualities such as tenderness, gentleness, kindness and concern, and also playfulness. We can distinguish warmth from protection giving. Also, one can have attachment in the absence of warmth–affection, and provide affectionate care for others (e.g., care of the dying) in the absence of (a desire for) attachment. Dominant animals and humans may be able to protect their infants from dangers and threats in a way that subordinates cannot (Suomi, 1999) but this does not mean that they provide more warmth. People may form attachments based on submission/appeasement to "not very warm others", if they see them as best bets for protection (Gilbert, 2005a). Indeed, anxiously attached people use appeasement as an attachment/security device (Sloman, 2000). Now, warmth is an important attribute of compassion—so what do we mean by "warmth"?

Warmth

There are a number of models that posit warmth as an important personality construct. It is linked to the agreeableness dimension in the "Big Five" personality trait classification, and the central love–hate dimension in the interpersonal circumplex model of personality (McCrae & Costa, 1989). Many studies have shown that "agreeable-warmth" attributes are associated with prosocial behaviour, better academic performance and well-being (e.g., Laursen, Pulkkinen, & Adams, 2002). It makes sense, then, that "warmth" should be a focus for therapeutic research and work.

Warmth appears to have at least three key attributes. First, warmth provides verbal and nonverbal signals of interest, caring and kindness that are *soothing*. Second, warmth can involve a sharing of positive affect between individuals that stimulates *liking*, affection and feelings of connectedness (in contrast to indifference, withdrawing or attacking). Third, warmth is more likely when individuals feel safe with each other and are trusting. Individuals who are easily threatened and become defensive may struggle to feel or express warmth.

Warmth underpins the positive feelings of soothing, calming and *being soothed*—it *moderates defensive emotions (anger, anxiety, sadness) and behaviours (e.g., aggression and flight)*, and can also turn off seeking, doing, achieving and acquiring. Part of the positive feelings of soothing may come from declines in, or regulations of, negative affect (e.g., feelings of relief; Gray, 1987). However, the positive affects of *social safeness-creating soothing*, via the exchange of *social signals*, that impact on the mind of the other, need consideration in their own right. This is because they have far-reaching organizing effects on the brain and are associated with specific social (safeness-conferring) signals (not just the removal of threat signals) such as nonverbal communication, facial expressions, voice tones and verbal content, and touch.

Field (2000) reviewed the evidence on the beneficial effects of holding, stroking and touching during development—interactions of affectionate care. Even laboratory rats grow up calmer if they are regularly stroked. These signals are soothing in their own right, and influence the release of endorphins. As Sapolsky (1994) observed:

> We readily think of stressors as consisting of various unpleasant things that can be done to an organism. Sometimes a stressor can be the *failure* to provide something to an organism, and the absence of touch is seemingly one of the most marked of developmental stressors that we can suffer.
>
> (p. 92)

So, from the first days of life, safeness-via-warmth is not simply the absence of threat but is *conferred* and stimulated by others with the soothing, care-giver signals of touching, stroking and holding (Field, 2000), voice tone, the "musicality" of the way a mother speaks to her child, positive/affectionate facial expressions, feeding and mutually rewarding interchanges that form the basis for the attachment *bond* (Trevarthen & Aitken, 2001). These signals stimulate endorphins that give rise to feelings of safeness, connectedness and *well-being*, and the infant's physiological systems are attuned to them (Carter, 1998; Wang, 2005). Thus, from birth, infants are highly sensitive to interpersonal communications and particular signals that regulate arousal, help organize physiological systems and set strategies onto developmental trajectories.

When we think about a "compassionate other" we normally imagine them as having qualities of low negative affect and generating warmth and expressing soothing signals (e.g., friendly facial expression and soothing voice with feelings in-them-about-us of acceptance). A basic co-regulating partnership, that involves genes and physiologies in one person communicating with genes and physiologies in another, and minds communicating with other minds, thus emerges. The very sense

55

of self is being sculptured in interaction, and at the root of this are brains that need others to love and care for them.

Hence, to "be socially soothed and feel safe" requires certain social signals, while to be "soothing" necessitates providing these signals to others (Gilbert, 1993, 2009a). As noted by Bowlby (1969, 1973) and Porges (2003, 2007), once soothed, individuals either may relax (passive safeness) or may redirect attention to explore the environment (active safeness). It has been this reasoning that has stimulated therapeutic work to try to teach people how to generate *soothing* (compassionate) images, feelings and thoughts (Gilbert, 2000a, 2009a; Gilbert & Irons, 2005). Interestingly, the same idea, of developing inner images of soothing others (e.g., bringing images of the compassionate Buddha to mind) is central to Buddhist compassion imagery (Vessantara, 1993). Importantly, for clinical work though, many high-shame clients find warmth and soothing difficult to do and are fearful and resistant of it (see Point 29)—as if this system is toned down and suppressed.

Validation seeking

Validation for emotions and personal reactions to (early) life events can be sought or avoided in therapy. Linehan (1993) and Leahy (2005) note the importance of emotion acceptance and validation of the child's emotions—a key process for compassion. Leahy outlined a useful model depicting how validation of emotions and early emotional coaching can link to different emotion strategies and relating styles. This is given in Figure 3. These styles will emerge in therapy and the therapeutic relationship.

When we develop the "the compassionate self" and engage in chair work (Points 21 and 22) we pay a lot of attention to the ability of the clients to be compassionately validating of their feelings and conflicts of feelings—which, for many, takes time to learn.

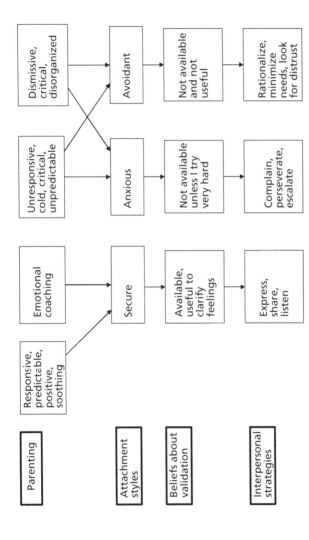

Figure 3 Relation of parenting, attachment styles, beliefs about validation and interpersonal strategies. Reproduced with kind permission from Gilbert, P. (ed.) (2005c) *Compassion: Conceptualisations, Research and Use in Psychotherapy.* London: Routledge

Cognitive abilities

Love and affection are like vitamins to the brain, but these go beyond physical interactions. There is increasing work showing that how a mother understands and responds to her child's emotions and needs is crucial to the child's ability to understand and regulate his/her own mind (Cozolino, 2007; Siegel, 2001; Wallin, 2007). So, in the context of validating, loving relationships, we come to feel safe and able to explore our own minds, to understand our emotions, to feel soothed and contained, and in the process are able to understand the minds of others. These cognitive abilities are vital for metacognitive abilities to be able reflect on our emotions, stand back from them and not be overwhelmed by them (Allen, Fonagy, & Bateman, 2008; Wallin, 2007; see Point 4).

Clarifying the CFT approach

As is evident from the above, CFT is rooted in the science of mind and basic psychological research in contrast to, say, a special "therapy focus". We also take a physiotherapy approach to mental health in the sense that the manifestation of a problem may not be the source of the problem. For example, I have had a problem in my lower back. Efforts to work on my lower back were only minimally helpful. Then a practitioner noticed that I was very flat-footed and my knees turn inwards, which affected my hips and put pressure on muscles in my back (what a wreck!). Without touching my back, but working on my flat-footed problem, he resolved the back difficulty. Sometimes psychotherapy can be like this too. If we only focus on trying to change the threat system we may fail to realize that part of the problem is in the balance of the other affect-regulation systems, and in particular the poor output from the soothing system. When that system is developed the others can settle down.

Philosophical position

The philosophical position of CFT arises from various observations on the nature of life. We call this a "reality check" and explore the challenges of life (Gilbert, 2009a). The "reality check" is used to offset pathologizing and is key to therapist training. These "reality checks" are as follows:

Evolved mind

We are an emergent species in the flow of life—part of mammalian and primate evolution. Our bodies, brains and minds evolved to function in specific ways with capacities for certain emotions (e.g., anger, anxiety, disgust, joy and lust), a range of defences (e.g., fight, flight and submission) and archetypal motivational systems (e.g., to form attachments, seek status, belong to groups, and desire and seek sexual partners). These are old brain motives and competences. They are the driving forces of much of what we do and think. Our "new brain" competencies and talents (for complex thinking, reflection and self-awareness) can interact with old brain motives and passions leading to the best and worst in ourselves. In different states of mind, different elements of our minds are turned on and off. The threat- or vengeance-focused mind often turns off motives and competencies for compassion to the targets of one's vengeance. In contrast, a "compassionate mind" tones down threat-focused feelings, thoughts and behaviours.

CFT begins, then, with the recognition that our brains are actually *difficult and tricky*; they are *not* well designed; our thoughts, emotions and behaviours can be captured by primitive emotions, motives—and terrors. In different mind states we think and feel quite differently. The Buddha took a similar view, suggesting that our minds are chaotic and craving, and that only through training our minds could we achieve some harmony within and take responsibility for ourselves and our actions.

Tragic mind

The second reality check is that our lives are relatively short (25,000–30,000 days, if we are lucky). We are caught in a genetic lottery, which determines the length of our lives and the kind of illnesses we will suffer. Young daughters, wives and mothers may die early due to breast-cancer genes. Leukaemia, cystic fibrosis or malaria can rob families of their children. We are subject to a huge range of illnesses that can cripple us, rob us of our capacities for hearing or sight or kill us slowly (e.g., AIDS, dementia). Humans have understood for a long time that in many ways we live a tragic life with much pain and suffering. Indeed, trying to explain why this should be has been at the root of many philosophical and spiritual traditions.

Compassion focused therapists work from a position of awareness of the "tragic mind". Indeed, it is the very real tragedies of our lives that summons up the importance of compassion; our common humanity and what we are all caught up in and are struggling with.

Social mind

The third reality check is the fact that we live in a world of immense injustice and suffering. We know that the social circumstances of our lives play a huge role in how our brains mature, the values that we develop, our motivations and the self-identities we grow into (Schore, 1994). Even our cognitive and mentalizing abilities are aided or stunted by the relation-ships that we grow up in (Allen et al., 2008; Cozolino, 2007). If I had been born into a Mexican drug cartel, or somehow there had been a baby swap at birth, the chances are I could now be dead, would have killed others, may be addicted to drugs myself and/or be living the rest of my life in prison. There would be no chance of the potential of what was in me (to become a professor of psychology and a clinician) ever coming to life in that environment. It is important to recognize and reflect on the fact that this "you" in "this life" is only "one version" of many that could have emerged the day you were born. When we look at our clients we are only seeing one aspect of their potential, only one version of that self—can we (see and) help them recognize and develop others?

From "not our fault" to taking responsibility

This shared understanding, about the predicament of our human minds and brains (and lives) leads to a recognition that much of what goes on in our minds is *not of our design and is*

61

therefore not our fault. Clarifying this aspect can play a key role in undermining a person's sense of being worthless, useless and no good when they become depressed or feel out of control of their minds. I have worked with groups of people diagnosed with severe borderline personality disorder and introduce them to the CFT model, explaining why much of what goes on in their brains is not their fault. We all *just find ourselves here*, with this difficult brain, created over millions of years of evolution, genetic dispositions and with a sense of ourselves and various emotional memories obtained through the social circumstances of our lives—none of which we chose. Although many of the people have undergone various types of therapy before, they usually say that no one had outlined this. We also discuss how "our coming to be ourselves" is the result of multiple factors (Gilbert, 2009b). Clients find this very de-shaming and reassuring at the beginning of therapy because many of them felt they were either bad or mad or had odd brains; that there was something very wrong with them for having the problems they had and this diagnosis. We say to clients, "We are not so interested in your diagnosis but we are very interested in how your threat, excitement and soothing systems are working for you". Time spent really helping people understand the "not our fault" aspect of our minds is time well spent because it orientates the person to approach their difficulties in a particular, more objective (compassionate) way.

However, this is only the beginning because it is easy to confuse "causality" with "responsibility", and so it is very important to distinguish these two. Therefore, we suggest to people that, "You might not be to blame for how your mind is, the passions, terrors and rages that can flow through it, but only you can take responsibility for training it for your and others' happiness. It is like a garden. You can leave your garden to grow and it will grow; weeds and flowers will grow but you may not like the tangles that emerge if you simply leave it to its own devices. Same with our minds. So, *cultivating, practising and focusing* on those elements of our minds that we wish to enhance is key if we are to take control over our minds". In many ways this is no different from saying to people that it may not be their fault that they are flat-footed, are short-sighted or suffer from a variety of complaints—but it is up to them to do something about it.

It can be useful, therefore, to encourage guided discovery and guided reflection on the unintended consequences of "not taking responsibility for change". However, keep in sight that that, too, is only one step because people are less likely to change just from threat, e.g., the threat of cancer may not stop people smoking. Rather, one must also build realistic images and pictures of the outcomes of change.

Key also in CFT is the de-shaming approach and ensuring that interventions stimulate particular systems. So, again, while it is important for clients to work at taking more and more responsibility for change, and to learn to tolerate setbacks without shaming, building the positive coping and compassionate self (see Point 21) gives a positive non-shaming focus for responsibility taking.

The interactions of new brain with old brain

In the standard CBTs the therapist tries to identify unhelpful thoughts, beliefs and schemas and then seeks to change the content of them. More recent therapies, such as Metacognitive Therapy (Fisher & Wells, 2009; Wells, 2000), Mindfulness (MBCT; Segal, Williams, & Teasdale, 2002), Dialectical Behaviour Therapy (DBT; Linehan, 1993) and Acceptance Commitment Therapy (ACT; Hayes et al., 2004), have all raised questions about the adequacy of this approach. They have focused instead on the nature of rumination and worry, and avoidance, and less on the content of cognitions. CFT suggests that both are important depending on case and context. For example, helping people with the contents of their beliefs, including those related to what is (un)necessary to stay safe, can be very helpful. However, we would add a shift to compassion

63

focusing first because it is not only the accuracy of alternatives that is key but also emotional experiences of them (see pages 164–165).

Clearly, too, attention to the ongoing processes of thoughts, linked to rumination, worry and self-criticism, are important. In CFT we argue that these processes operate as complex stimulators of the three (old brain) affect-regulation systems, activate physiological systems and fuel certain mentalities. For example, feeling put down or disrespected and having angry and vengeful rumination maintains the threat system *and* the competitive mentality; ruminating on lack of love or affiliative bonds maintains the threat system *and* the care-seeking mentality.

In Metacognitive Therapy, Wells (2000; Fisher & Wells, 2009) makes clear that rumination (looking back) and worry (looking forward) exert their impact when they constantly stimulate the threat system, and interfere with normal recovery processes. In this approach, problems arise because attention is overly focused on the self and threat to the self from within and without; this sense of threat is maintained through rumination and worry; and self-regulation strategies fail to modify this processing loop and the self-experiences (e.g., inferiority or vulnerability beliefs) that give rise to it. In CFT we would suggest that self-regulation strategies (also) fail because they're not linked into the appropriate affect-regulation system. Thus, it is not so much the content of cognition but the repetition of threat-focused thinking that is harmful. Attention reallocation is therefore a key element of this intervention. CFT suggests that it is also useful to try to stimulate the natural regulator of the threat-protection system—the soothing and affiliative system—using compassionate refocusing, imagery and attention (see Part 2).

The key point in Wells' approach, and in those that focus on mentalizing, is that problematic emotions and difficulties are maintained *because of the creation of an internal feedback loop* between the content and focus of one's thoughts and the threat system. Keep in mind that the threat system is not designed for

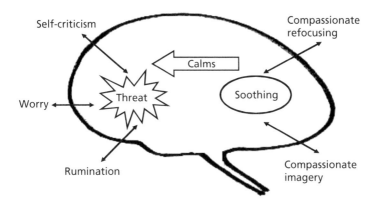

Figure 4 Stimulating different systems

complex thinking but for rapid actions and, therefore, CFT suggests it makes sense to try to shift to a different affect system in order to facilitate new processing.

This can be depicted simply, as in Figure 4. Arrows go both ways because the more threatened we feel the more our attention and thinking becomes threat focused, and the more threat-linked intrusions we might experience. The point is that self-criticisms, worries and ruminations that are constantly circulating in one's mind are also constantly stimulating threat-based central (brain) and peripheral systems (e.g., the sympathetic and parasympathetic nervous systems). Over time these pathways become stronger.

In this context, therefore, CFT sees the mechanisms of change as:

1   to disengage from the (inner) stimulators of threat, e.g., ruminative, self-criticalness or anger (shared with metacognitive- and mindfulness-based therapies), and refocus on compassion insights and feelings;

65

2 to be able to compassionately "stand back" from one's inner storms of emotion and become more "observant and watching" of one's thoughts and feelings "as they arise" rather than caught up in them (as in mindfulness- and acceptance-based therapies)—having a compassion base can help that difficult process;

3 to activate the natural threat regulator in the brain—the soothing system—by switching to compassionate refocusing and imagery;

4 to be able to engage with aversive inner experiences, such as trauma memory, or avoided emotions, by first developing an inner compassion base.

Rumination and goals

Rumination is often linked to goals and feeling thwarted (Klinger, 1977), so in CFT rumination often requires functional analysis on goals. For example, ruminating after making a mistake can be linked to a threat-fear of being seen as incompetent and rejected; so rumination can be linked to activity in the incentive and resource-seeking system (wanting to succeed). CFT helps people recognize that they may have to make changes in their lives, give up things, come to terms with losses, realign their goals and sense of self, engage with things that frighten them—all of which require courage. In CFT we talk a lot about the development of courage—and that this is more likely if we can create kind, helpful and supportive voices in our heads rather than coldly logical, bullying, critical or pushy ones.

So, in a whole range of interventions a compassion focus textures that intervention, but the interventions themselves are taken from a range of different evidence-based therapies.

Formulation

Case formulation is an individualized process that seeks to understand the nature, sources, maintaining factors and alleviation factors for people's difficulties (Eells, 2007; Tarrier, 2006). Many therapists recognize that case formulation needs to be embedded within the person's past and current context and should be based on an understanding of the *functions* of that person's emotions, behaviour and thoughts (Cullen & Combes, 2006). Two people may take an overdose—one was depressed, the other drunk and lost count of the painkillers taken for a hangover. The meaning of a depression in someone who, on the surface at least, appears to have a relatively good marriage and job is quite different from a depression in the context of poverty and domestic violence or previous child sexual abuse. Even though both people may have similar symptoms and beliefs of "being weak and a failure" when depressed, their beliefs may have very different origins and functions.

Nearly all psychotherapies believe that symptoms of mental-health difficulties revolve around threat, and mechanisms of defence and protection (Gilbert, 1993). Psychoanalysis derives a complex set of *internal* defences, such as repression, projection, denial and sublimation. CBT also focuses on issues of threat and defence but uses behavioural frameworks, where avoidance is a primary defensive behaviour. In a number of writings Salkovskis (e.g., 1996) outlined various behaviours linked to the avoidance of aversive outcomes (Thwaites & Freeston, 2005). He makes clear that (counter to how it is sometimes portrayed) CBT *is not* about showing people that they are being irrational or erroneous in their thinking, but about investigating how and where they have got stuck and trapped in understandable but unhelpful ways of trying, as best they can, to make sense of their problems and to get (or stay) safe. He points out that people often develop beliefs around safety behaviours that strengthen rather than test out or weaken those same beliefs. For example, a panic client may sit down because they think they could have a heart attack. When the heart attack does not come they do not attribute its absence to their erroneous belief but to the fact that they sat down. Safety behaviours therefore become entrenched by: (1) experienced short-term benefits/reinforcers (e.g., relief); and (2) beliefs that maintain them. Safety behaviours and strategies are aimed at avoiding both *external* and *internal* threats/harms and are therefore *key threat–self-protection (system) regulators*. For example, a socially anxious person may monitor their verbal output, speak little in order to avoid appearing stupid, and constantly try to work out how they appear in the minds of other people. This is to avoid the external threat of rejection, exclusion or humiliation. In order to control their *internal* threat of anxiety arising, and just feeling bad, they may drink alcohol.

CFT only has three basic emotion-regulation systems to work with and so formulation is around the organization of these systems with a particular focus on threat and safety strategy *development*. Moreover, CFT suggests that there are a number of innate and evolved potential safety strategies that can be activated and texture self-evaluative systems (Gilbert, 2001a). For example, a child who we will call Ann who is regularly threatened by her parents may come to monitor the aggressive state of mind of the parent and quickly adopt submissive or avoidance strategies if she picks up cues of threat. The submissive and avoidance strategies are a *normal* part of an innate repertoire of social defences. As Ann grows up, with increasing cognitive competencies for self–other awareness coming on line, theses experiences, of the activation of safety strategies, form part of her *self-experience and identity*. So, for example, when confronted with a powerful other, Ann will automatically monitor their state of mind and herself to make sure she is not doing things to stir up their anger. If anger is directed at her, she will then try to work out what it was she did (self-blame) and adopt submissive strategies to minimize the threat. So, automatic defensive strategies become linked to cognitive systems such that people quickly self-monitor, self-blame, and behave submissively. In addition, they will, of course, have beliefs about the self to match these strategies, such as seeing themselves as weak, blameworthy and so forth. In CFT we would make clear these are developed *safety* protection strategies rather than use the language of cognitive distortions, and spend time helping the person understand their function and the *fear* of changing. It is these unique profiles of safety strategies, which arise from threat and unmet needs, that are important in CFT, rather than a more diagnostic approach of trying to identify specific symptoms, core beliefs or schemas.

Key elements of a CFT formulation

The CFT formulation for high-shame and self-critical people integrates cognitive, behavioural and attachment models and focuses on four key domains:

1 innate and historical influences that give rise to—
2 key external and internal threats and fears that give rise to—
3 externally focused and internally focused safety strategies that give rise to—
4 unintended consequences—that fuel more distress, safety strategies and difficulties—including self-criticism.

The unintended problems/consequences can be related to symptoms, which then give rise to a fifth aspect (say) of fear, anger and various metacognitions about how one is currently (not) coping and is suffering (e.g., depressed or anxious).

Background and historical influences

Here the therapist explores for basic early relating and attachment styles, life events and emotional memories, that illuminate issues of feeling cared for or about, or neglected, unmet needs, experiences of feeling threatened and forms of abuse. The latter may only emerge slowly and depends on the person feeling safe enough to be able to tell of these events. We know, for example, that many people can go through therapy, and due to shame, do not reveal key issues for them (e.g., MacDonald & Morley, 2001; Swan & Andrews, 2003). Given this, therapists who rely on "problem lists" in therapy may be at most risk of missing shame problems.

Early life experiences will have patterned various neurophysiological systems and the co-ordination of various affect-regulation systems (Cozolino, 2007; Ogden, Minton, & Pain, 2006). We now know, for example, that early care (or a lack of it, or abuse) affects brain maturation, affect regulation (Gerhardt, 2004; Schore, 1994, 2001; Siegel, 2001), cognitive abilities, and abilities to mentalize and understand other people's thoughts and feelings (Allen et al., 2008; Siegel, 2001). The therapist explores for key emotional memories that act as a focus for self-experience and can be triggered by life events (Brewin, 2006).

Some people, however, may have poor recall of negative events, go blank or find revealing and "going into the history" stressful. Others will tell that "all was wonderful" and it is only later that you find out it was not. The importance of the coherence of a narrative of one's background has been illuminated by research on attachment using the Adult Attachment Interview (Mikulincer & Shaver, 2007). So we know that it is important to ask specific questions. "You felt that mum/dad loved you—*how* did she/he show this? *How* did she/he comfort you; *how* did she/he talk to you about your feelings? *In what ways* were they physically affectionate; if you were distressed *how* would they help you?" Commonly, in shame-based problems you will find the absence of feelings of closeness, validation and support, and not uncommonly experiences of distance and threats/harms.

Careful history taking emerges over time because it is not just "fact finding" and identifying "hot spots" (that were a spur for safety strategies and developing personal meanings) but it also offers key opportunities to compassionately empathize and validate people's life experiences (Leahy, 2005; Linehan, 1993). Creating "safeness" in these ways, enables people to develop a coherent story and narrative of their difficulties. Therapy may be the first time people have experienced another person's mind orientated to them in this interested, non-judgemental, containing, empathic and caring way and it helps them to create a coherent (de-shaming) narrative (Gilbert, 2007b). This begins the process of people beginning to understand their problems in terms of phenotypic development, a mind that has been orientated to "better safe than sorry" and "safety first" life strategies, with a sense of self being textured by these experiences.

Emotional memories of the self

It is important to explore the felt sense of self and understand how this is linked to emotional memories. For example, Gilbert (2003) suggested:

Consider early experiences of how a child experiences *the emotions of others* in an interaction and these become the foundations for self-beliefs. A positive belief of, "I am a lovable competent person" is really shorthand for, "in my memory systems are many emotionally textured experiences of *having elicited positive emotions in others* and being treated in a loving way, and as competent—therefore I am lovable". Suppose parents are often angry towards a child. This child develops beliefs that others do not see her positively, which is shorthand for, "in my memory systems are emotionally textured experiences of *having elicited anger in others* and being treated as bad—therefore I am bad". Suppose parents

71

always show contempt or withdraw their love and turn away from the child. It is not anger that is internalised but loss or contempt. This child develops beliefs that others see her as someone to turn away from and believes she is unlovable. This is shorthand for "in my memory systems are emotionally textured experiences *of having elicited withdrawal in others* and being treated as undesirable—therefore I am undesirable". Consider the child who is sexually abused. This can become, "in my memory systems are emotionally textured experiences of fear and disgust—therefore I am, disgusting and bad". Tomkins (1987) argued that shame (and other self-conscious emotions) are laid down in memory as scenes and fragments of images of self in relationships. These encoded scenes can then become "mini co-ordinators" of attention, thinking, feeling and behaviour—giving rise to what Jung called "complexes".

(pp. 1221–1222)

Psychodynamic therapists would see these processes as "self-objects", cognitive therapists as "self-schemas". The key point, though, is that schemas of self emerge from self–other inter-actions and are rooted in emotional memories, which can affect body memory and the "felt sense of self" (Brewin, 2006; Ogden et al., 2006). This is why, when working with shame, CFT often works directly with the core experiences (e.g., of threat and aloneness–sadness, see Points 10 and 11), revisiting threat memories and developing new compassionate–safe emotional experiences (Hackmann, 2005; Lee, 2005). Working only on the explicit processing systems by trying to develop rational alternatives to shame may not be sufficient to influence emotion laden memories that fuel and maintain a defensive orientation (Brewin, 2006).

Key threats, fears and unmet needs

Early background experiences can enable us to feel safe and secure or easily threatened and insecure (Mikulincer & Shaver,

2007). As Gilbert (1989), Beck et al. (2003) and other therapies note, key fears arising in childhood, which are going to have long-term influence, are often around archetypal and innate themes of abandonment, disengagement, rejection, shame and abuse/harm. In CFT we distinguish between *external* threats and *internal* threats. External threats pertain to what the world or others might do; whereas internal threats are related to what emerges, or is recreated inside oneself. For example, a person might be frightened of *the external threats of* rejection, exploitation or harm from others; and/or of *the internal threats* of losing control or becoming overwhelmed by anxiety, anger or depression (internal threat). Indeed, it can be the fear of becoming depressed (again) that can set in motion rumination, avoidance, fear and dread of the future and even suicide (Gilbert, 2007a). Helping people articulate and reflect on what key fears and concerns they might be carrying from childhood can be immensely helpful—especially when we look at the next element, which is how they will have tried to protect themselves from childhood onwards—setting in place their protective strategies and shields. Indeed, all the time we talk in terms of what difficult backgrounds generate in us, then the need to develop "safety strategies", "efforts at self-protection", "what did you need to get good at", and how one ends up "doing the best one could at the time".

Safety and compensatory strategies

From the first days of life our brains automatically develop a range of strategies to seek safety, self-protect and self-soothe. There are genetic differences in the disposition of infants and children to engage in certain strategies. For example, some children are more easy to soothe and comfort with physical affection than others. Shy children are more wary and avoidant than more explorative children. Some children are able to use their parents as a safe base whereas for others the parents are themselves a source of threat (Liotti, 2000). There is also now much research on how children respond to threats by using their parents as sources of reference (is this safe or not?—as in the visual-cliff experiments), protection and calming (Mikulincer & Shaver, 2007). While some children turn easily and expectantly to their parents for calming when threatened, others are far more avoidant, with a third type being orientated to the parents but not able to calm down when held or soothed. All of this speaks to the regulation of the threat system.

Parents are so important to a child's safety that children will try to influence the mind of their parents (Liotti, 2000, 2002; Wallin, 2007). They may become very submissive, or competitive and striving, or caring and rescuing, polite and well mannered. These safety strategies have a hope that others can be encouraged to be helpful and value them. If more externalizing safety strategies, such as aggression and impulsiveness, develop there seems to be a turning away (of hope) of building affiliative relationships in favour of more self-reliant, protective strategies and of ensuring that one's potential to be harmful registers in the mind of others so that they remain wary of one. This is a strategy (of suddenly being aggressive) that some dominant monkeys use to maintain fear in subordinates (Gilbert & McGuire, 1998).

Humans evolved to require caring attachments, to be looked after and soothed when stressed. Deviations from these developmental trajectories have consequences. Unmet needs can constitute a threat in that the individual is not able to develop optimally without specific inputs. This can lead to a certain *yearning and seeking* and various fears that certain types of relationship cannot be obtained or maintained (Knox, 2003). Along with this go complex safety and compensatory strategies. For example, a girl who has a poor relationship with her father, or turns to him to protect her from (say) a cold mother, may have a yearning to form a close relationship with a father figure and find herself attracted to older males who may or may not be helpful attachment figures. Given the functions parents have, such as protection, provisioning, soothing, validation, encouraging, "delighting in the achievements of", these can all be sought in the therapeutic relationship—or indeed from other people. When the person finds they are not forthcoming in the way that they want, they can feel thwarted again, threatened and disappointed.

Unintended consequences

It is basic to CBT that safety strategies nearly always have unintended and often undesirable consequences; "symptoms" being one of them (Salkovskis, 1996; Stott, 2007; Thwaites & Freeston, 2005). These consequences can also either maintain the problem or make it much worse. For example, individuals who are frightened of their emotions (e.g., some emotions trigger internal threat) may engage in experiential avoidance—a key focus in various exposure therapies, such as ACT, and also Mindfulness (Hayes et al., 2004). Fear of the impact that revealing or expressing their emotions might have on others can lead to avoiding openness and honesty in relationships. As a result the relationship lacks self-correcting interactions (e.g., sharing dissatisfactions) and the person begins to ruminate more and more on the unspoken resentments. These ruminations are depressing and usually people become poor at identifying the real difficulties and solutions or, on the other hand, acknowledging what they like and appreciate. In an effort to try to maintain a positive relationship by being submissive and hiding negative feelings, unintended consequences have actually produced the feared event. The person may then conclude that they are not lovable because of some characteristic and may not recognize that it's their safety behaviours that are causing trouble.

The link between threats, safety strategies and unintended consequences can be complex. For example, David grew up in an emotionally deprived background linked to the death of a young sibling. He grew up in an atmosphere where "terrible things just happen". His mother was frequently distressed and aggressive. It took us some time to work out that he ran a strategy of "better never to hope of feeling positive about oneself because it can all be dashed". He could recall many times when he might feel positive about himself but then the anger and criticism of his mother would give him "a dreadful heart-sinking feeling", and a sense that he'd been "completely wrong to feel positive". He developed a life set of strategies of deliberately trying to avoid stimulating his positive affect system and simply keep his head down and out of trouble. It took some time for him to recognize that unless he stimulated his positive affect systems it would be near impossible to get out of depression. He demonstrated a clear fear of positive emotion, positive feelings about the self, and an inability to turn to others. In his work he was known as a very reliable person who would always "step in". He became aware, however, that this was not because he wanted to take responsibility but felt that if he didn't, he couldn't trust other people to do a good job. He wasn't frightened of being abandoned or rejected; he was frightened that there was no one good enough to take responsibility, sort things out and it would "all end in disaster". You can imagine the serious transference issues this gave us!

Clearly, in this short book we can't go into the details of these complex linkages, but if therapists focus with a very clear Socratic method on guided discovery and look to the individual and *unique patterns* of threat and self-protection in a person's life, such themes will emerge. That's why in CFT we encourage people not to try to identify specific issues or core beliefs in advance as if ticking off on a checklist, but rather have unique formulations based on complex functional analysis and reflective narratives—all around the three circles (Point 6).

Although various therapists talk about helping clients to recognize that they have often been doing "unhelpful things for good reasons", it is important to have a very *clear emotionally connected* understanding of the link between specific safety strategies and early life events. It is when people make *emotional* connections that change can occur—and sometimes these connections can be very moving. In other words, don't "just say things"; ensure your client emotionally connects to it. Consider Susan who is very angry with herself:

Paul: Susan, as I understand it, when your mother was taking drugs and alcohol, that was frightening for you and when frightened you'd hide in your room, feeling very alone [*pause and space*]—but at the same time you wanted to be closer to mum. Drifting into drugs yourself makes perfect sense because it seems to me you were trying to find a way to connect with people, and feel better yourself—and of course get some release from the lonely despair you had felt for so long [*Pause and space*]. Getting into drugs *was not your fault*. It was the part of you that was trying to work it out, how to feel better and connect with people—to do the best you could.

Susan: Yes but I should have known. I saw the mess drugs had made of her f***ing life. I was stupid—so f***ing stupid.

Paul: [*Very slowly and gently*] Look at me Susan, this was not your fault, you felt so alone didn't you. It was not your fault. Had you been born into another family you would not have walked that path.
            [*Goes quiet a long time so I repeat slowly*] It was not your fault.

Susan: [*Susan is now tearful*] Oh, I guess so, part of me didn't want to go down that road yet another part was desperate to do so; I just wanted to join in and connect with some people—anyone. I had been around druggies all my life so they felt like my people in a way, people who would accept me and I was like them.

Susan both loved and was very angry with her mother, but to work on that we first moved a step to giving up self-anger and towards how to change. In CFT, once we get hold of the anger and shame then we are much more likely to be able to compassionately work on change. It will be a back and forth process though. In shame it is important to *emotionally* connect with blaming and self-condemnation, and not be vague about "good reasons" for problematic behaviour.

Formulation on those four basic aspects, can naturally lead to insight into how one's symptoms have emerged as natural consequences of early background and safety strategies. We are out of the domain of pathologizing and labelling and into the domain of understanding and recognizing why much of what's happening inside the people we are working with "is not their fault"—how people have got unintentionally trapped in their ways of thinking and behaviour (Salkovkis, 1996). This view, when clearly communicated, along with the evolutionary model, can do much to eat away at the roots of shame and self-criticism.

Formulation and the circles

In addition, formulation can also be discussed in terms of the three circles (see Point 6). Here the client is invited to think about each system/circle and reflect on how each works for them. How big are the circles relative to each other? How does each work? What life factors may have influenced their development? How do they regulate each other? What kinds of things would they put into them? Commonly clients feel that their threat system seems to be bigger than their drive–pleasure or contentment/affiliative and soothing systems. They may immediately see that they use achievements and striving to compensate for threats—or that they are not open to kindness from others, and are more critical than kind to themselves. So, you can ask people to draw each of their three circles in terms of how much they operate within them, how powerful they are for them or how well developed they are. These pictorial representations can be useful for offering insight, planning therapeutic interventions and independent practice. It also helps to explore and reflect together that perhaps the threat and self-protection system has become overdeveloped for understandable reasons.

Formulation is not one process

In CFT there are ongoing and different formulation processes that unfold in a series of steps. These can be outlined as follows:

First formulation

- Presentation of current problems and symptoms.
- Validating and making sense of current difficulties.
- Establishing the therapeutic relationship—noting potential difficulties.

Second formulation

- Exploring cultural and historical context.
- Narrating life history and story.
- Gaining insight into key emotional memories of self and other (self–other schema).

Third formulation

- Structured formulating in the context of the model's four domains of: background; threats, fears, concerns and unmet needs; internal and external safety and compensatory strategies; and unintended consequences.
- Identifying particularly problematic safety and affect-regulation strategies, such as avoidance, rumination, substance use or self-harm.

Fourth formulation

- Explaining the model (evolved mind).
- Distinguishing between "not your fault" and "responsibility taking".
- Explaining the "three circles"—and reformulating in those terms.
- Outlining the "brain diagram" (see page 146).

Fifth formulation

- Formulating the therapeutic tasks, e.g., thought monitoring and generating alternatives, behavioural experiments or graded tasks, developing "the compassionate self", compassionate imagery and letter writing.
- Exploring blocks and difficulties.

Sixth formulation

- Revisiting earlier formulations in light of progress on tasks and new information.
- Developing and adjusting therapeutic tasks.
- Future work together and then beyond therapy.
- Life practice.
- Preparing for ending.

These are obviously for *general guidance* only, not necessarily unfolding in this order in some linear mechanistic manner, and there may be a number of other subformulations. So, although these are outlined as a linear sequence, things may not be as neat as that. People may move through the different steps at different speeds and go back and forth. The point is, formulation is an ongoing process that focuses on different elements of the therapeutic journey (Eells, 2007). Keep in mind, too, that through all this process there will be variations in the client's ability to mentalize and stand back from and reflect on what's going on in their minds and in the therapy. These variations in mentalizing competencies will impact on your therapy. So some assessment of these abilities is important for your formulation and treatment plan.

In addition, formulation will include and clarify "treatment goals" and outcomes. Understanding, working and shaping together the client's goals and objectives, including those linked to self-identity (e.g., to develop one's compassionate self), act as a key focus for intervention. This is different to only being symptom focused.

10

Shame

Concerns with self-evaluation and self-feelings are central to many psychological therapies but few locate their therapy within the shame literature and science of self-conscious emotion—about which we now know a fair amount (Tracy, Robins, & Tangney, 2007). Understanding and working with the complexities of shame plays a major role in CFT. The CFT model of shame (see Figure 5) is linked to the fact that humans have evolved to want to create positive feelings about the self in the mind of others (see Gilbert, 2007c). It suggests that:

1   We are all born with the need to connect to other minds and feel cared for. This blossoms into desires to socially connect in one's group; to find acceptance and social belonging to facilitate helpful relationships; to be wanted, appreciated and valued (Gilbert, 1989; Hrdy, 2009). If we achieve this then our worlds are much safer (and our threat systems settle) in contrast to not being valued or wanted, rejected or struggling alone. Helpful relationships are physiologically regulating (Baumeister & Leary, 1995).
2   The way that we experience our intimate relationships—as either caring or neglectful and abusive; and our peer relationships—as either caring and accepting or rejecting and abusive, has a major impact on how we experience "ourselves" as living in the minds of others. To be vulnerable to external shame is to be sensitive to negative feelings and thoughts about the self *in the mind of others*. So, working out how one exists for others is fundamental to our feelings of safeness in the world. Hence, external shame is at the centre of this model (see Figure 5).

COMPASSION FOCUSED THERAPY

3 There are two major defences (safety strategies) to external shame. One is the internalized shaming response where one adopts a subordinate, submissive strategy associated with self-monitoring and self-blaming. The other is an externalizing, humiliated response where one adopts a more dominant aggressive, attacking response—one tries to create a sense of personal security via one's ability to overpower or bully potential attackers/rejecters. These are not consciously chosen strategies but reflect phenotypic variations, and they can be context dependent.

4 Reflected shame is related to the shame others can bring on you by your association with them and shame you bring to others. This can be especially important in some cultural

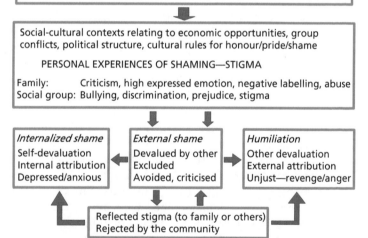

Figure 5 An evolutionary and biopsychosocial model for shame. Adapted from Gilbert, P. (2002) "Evolutionary approaches to psychopathology and cognitive therapy", in P. Gilbert (ed.) Special Edition: Evolutionary Psychology and Cognitive Therapy, *Cognitive Psychotherapy: An International Quarterly*, 16: 263–294

contexts, for example it is associated with honour killings (Gilbert, Gilbert, & Sanghera, 2004c).

Like other models, CFT distinguishes between fears and beliefs about the *external* social world (what others think about and can do to the self) and *internal* fears and beliefs (e.g., fear of one's own "inadequacies", failures or losing control to one's own emotions, fantasies or thoughts). Although there is an obvious overlap and interaction between "externally" focused threat and "internally" focused threat, CFT clarifies this distinction with clients repeatedly because both the coping behaviours (protection–safety strategies) and interventions vary as to the focus of the threat. So, it is useful to clearly separate out the two types of thinking. For example, the break up of a romantic relationship may result in much grief but when shame is involved there are two other streams of thoughts. Here is an example of Tim:

External shame	*Internal shame*
Attention and reasoning focused on what is going on in the minds of others about the self as object.	Attention and reasoning focused inwardly on one's experience of self as subject.
This relationship broke up because Sally went off me.	I often feel anxious and uncertain what to say or do. I become confused and vulnerable. I worry that my anxiety will stop me doing what I want to do.
She sees me as boring and anxious. She was nice but she was probably thinking for some time of how to end it.	This is rather pathetic. I am pathetic.

My key fear is:	*My key fear is*:
That in the minds of others I exist as a boring, wallpaper person; not able to elicit love and affection—destined to be alone.	Being unable to change or cope with anxiety and being stuck as an undesirable self. Stuck with feelings of being alone and miserable; an unwanted nobody.
(Reactivation of childhood memory of experience of others.)	(Reactivation of childhood memory of inner experience of self.)

There is usually a link between external and internal shame and when written down separately people can often see this—i.e., that the way they think others think about them is often how they think/feel about themselves. One can explain that this is linked to projection and how, when we feel threatened, projection is more likely, because of "better safe than sorry" thinking (Gilbert, 1998), creating a vicious circle.

Note also that we focus on key fears/threats. We use the term "key fears/threats" rather than, say, "bottom line" (which is sometimes used in CBT) because we want to use language that links directly to the threat system. Also, we want to link this to basic, evolved and archetypal fears of rejection and fears of "being unable to influence the minds of others in one's favour". We can then explore a functional analysis of the self-critical inner dialogue because, as related to threat, the external focus will have a different function to the internal focus. The functions of thoughts related to external threat are often about warnings and explanations, e.g., "People won't like you because . . .; you are vulnerable to . . .; you are not making good impressions in the minds of others . . .; if you don't change/stop/control . . . then . . .; you must stop being miserable because people won't like you . . .". These are common, involuntary subordinate concerns.

Note that the protection–safety behaviours can be similar or quite different for external and internal shame. To control his anxiety a man might drink alcohol before he goes to see his girlfriend. To impress her, however, he might buy a car that he cannot really afford. Thus, the way we cope with fears emanating from the inner and outer world can be different.

There are two different types of shamed-linked trauma that can activate the threat system. The first is the obvious one of abuse. These are traumas of *intrusion* where another person (or people) has violated the control and boundaries of the person and been highly threatening/hurtful. The other traumas are those of being *too distant* from others, commonly where others have been hard to please or elicit affection from and there has been an absence of affection; the shame of not being good enough to be selected or wanted (see Dugnan, Trower, & Gilbert, 2002, for concepts and a scale to measure them).

Shame of exclusion

The shame here is related to feeling one is rarely noticed or wanted—it is not so much active rejection as passive ignoring. One client said, "I loved mum, but she worked hard and there were always more important things for her to do. I guess I just wasn't important enough for her". These folk can come to constantly feel not "interesting or attractive or good enough", can become strivers in an effort to find ways to feel connected to others—but their successes rarely satisfy those searches (see Point 14). The example of Tim above could be linked to an exclusion type of shame and anxiety.

Intrusion and violation shame

For those who suffer the intrusions of others, they can feel powerless to stop or defend against "the other" doing things *to* them and are rendered small, powerless and frightened. One can experience the self as an object "to be used" by the other.

Verbal abuse and shaming is *injecting* negative meanings/labels into experiences of the self. In evolutionary terms such indoctrinations are regarded as memes (basic ideas and beliefs) that act like viruses/infections, replicating themselves inside the person and indeed in relationships (Blackmore, 1996). There is some evidence that verbal abuse and having one "self" defined by others in negative terms can be as powerful and pathogenic as physical and sexual abuse (Teicher, Samson, Polcari, & McGreenery, 2006). Indeed, one sometimes hears stories like, "Well I could cope with the beatings if I knew mum/dad loved me—it was when they called me stupid and 'a useless bastard' and I felt they did not like, let alone love me, that really dug deep into me. If your own flesh and blood don't love or want you then I guess you are pretty useless". Peer shaming can also have a significant impact on one's sense of self as a social agent, and vulnerability to shame and self-criticism (Gibb, Abramson, & Alloy, 2004).

Shame memory

There is increasing evidence that shame memories can act like trauma ones, involving intrusiveness, hyperarousal, efforts to avoid shame feeling (Matos & Pinto-Gouveia, in press), and, of course, shame can have a major impact on our sense of ourselves and who and how we engage socially (Gilbert, 2007c). To explore the complexities of shame and trauma *memory* we can look at a case example.

Case study

Sara came from a poor family, whose mother had "a number of partners" and suffered from alcohol abuse. Her mother was unpredictable and often verbally and physically aggressive. Sara had *many* trauma memories but one was from about seven or eight. She recalls feeling relatively happy, playing with her friends in the corridor of the house, making "giggly" noises. Her mother was drunk and "came flying out of the room" where she had been sleeping and hit Sara about the head making her nose bleed and cut her lip. She also screamed at Sara that she was a bad selfish girl for "waking mother up with her stupid, f***ing games". Her friends were alarmed and fled the scene immediately leaving Sara completely alone, overwhelmed with fear, terror and sadness, and the pain of being hit. She recalls her body "crouched and shaking".

The conditioning implications of this are clear. Tomkins (1987) pointed out that shame memories are *scenes in our minds*, an interlinked set of body-based feelings and events that are sources *of emotional conditioning*. It is vital to engage with this complexity.

In Sara's, emotional memory will be:

1   the inner cues of having fun (inner positive affect);
2   associated with an intense raging (external) attack;
3   associated with self-defining verbal labels (stupid, selfish);
4   associated with friends running away and being left completely alone;
5   associated with pain and shock at being hit;
6   associated with her own defence system automatically creating in her body patterns of submissive, fearful/ terrorized, crouching and shaking.

After the attack Sara is sent to her room to be alone. At the very time that a child needs comfort and care (when they are very distressed and frightened) Sara has been isolated. It is no wonder that she is overwhelmed by feelings of *aloneness* when she becomes distressed because of *conditioned emotional memories*. In addition, there are feelings of *entrapment* because there is no way she can get away from her mother—go and live

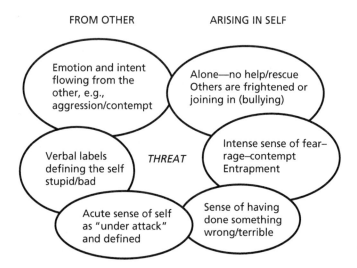

FROM OTHER   ARISING IN SELF

Emotion and intent flowing from the other, e.g., aggression/contempt

Alone—no help/rescue
Others are frightened or joining in (bullying)

Verbal labels defining the self stupid/bad

THREAT

Intense sense of fear–rage–contempt
Entrapment

Acute sense of self as "under attack" and defined

Sense of having done something wrong/terrible

Figure 6 Associations of threat "meanings" in shame-traumas

somewhere else. And even those desires might be internally alarming for her. In CFT we try to capture these complexities of emotional memory.

An example of these interlocking processes is offered in Figure 6.

This diagram is simply to help you work with your clients so that you can see the awareness of emotions in "the other", what arises in the self including verbal labels and fears, and the experience in these cases of feeling trapped and *very alone*. Not only did no one come to rescue your client from the abuse (and this may include sexual abuse), but afterwards she/he was left alone with no soothing from the outside.

As an aside, I grew up in Africa in the outback and these things wouldn't happen. If the parent was angry with the child or even hit them, the child would run off to a grandmother or an aunt—they wouldn't be left alone in a room! (see also Hrdy, 2009). One can also see how and why Sara may become very attentive to certain feelings *in herself* (e.g., fun) that will automatically trigger a fear of punishment and a sense of doing something wrong, a sense of being alone in a frightening world and wanting to curl up and hide. Classical conditioning is the model CFT refers to here.

In CFT the experience of aloneness, being cut off from a source of affiliative soothing when distressed, is a central experience to work with. You might also draw out another set of circles looking at what could not be processed in that (frightened) brain state, e.g., rage at mother, or a desire to heal mother or abandon her, or have her locked away, and the possible fears of acknowledging these possibilities or sense of betrayal (Gilbert & Irons, 2005). Indeed, Sara wanted her mother arrested by the police, but felt very frightened of acknowledging these feelings because at times her mother could be loving. Hence, she was a feared and wanted object—which really scrambles the attachment system—wanting to be soothed by someone who has threatened you. These issues, and their relation to disorganized attachment and mentalizing difficulties, have been explored by Liotti and Prunetti (2010).

CFT might also tap grief for the mother/parent one so dearly wanted—the personal archetypal mother/parent. This is not commonly considered in CBT therapies but can be extremely important—even though in one sense one is grieving for a fantasy (Gilbert & Irons, 2005). Indeed, the abilities to grieve and work through complex grief-linked emotions might aid the development of mentalizing.

Hence, rather than tackle this at the level of a belief (in, say, inferiority, vulnerability or defectiveness) or automatic thoughts, one would *unpack* these experiences coded in the threat system; break them down into their core components. These are fear of the other, arousal of inner fear, a sense of aloneness, and verbal labels in the experience—of being stupid. After clarifying the different components in this memory (that might fuel a core belief), one can then: (1) explore how Sara's brain will (for self-protective reasons) automatically try to develop defensive strategies; and (2) work out a compassionate intervention for *each* aspect.

The many influences of shame

Shame can be focused on various aspects of self, such as one's body, feelings, fantasises and desires, past behaviours, and personal characteristics. Shame can also play a major role in:

1   the acquisition of vulnerability to emotional distress;
2   the development of sense of self;
3   coping behaviours and safety strategies;
4   lack of openness to others, unable to identify with others (the only one), avoid help seeking—including whether to come for therapy or not;
5   coping with in-session feelings and process (e.g., being overwhelmed with tears, losing control, or revealing abuse) and whether to drop out or not;
6   how they react in therapy overall, including shaming that might be happening at home as clients try to change; and
7   what they reveal or keep hidden.

Anyone working with complex cases would do well to understand the many complexities of shame. Another complexity is self-criticism.

Self-criticism

Self-criticism is very common in shame. Self-criticism has been associated with a range of mental-health difficulties and in psychosis about 70% of voices are hostile and critical (Gilbert & Irons, 2005). Self-criticism has various origins and functions. Figure 7 offers a brief model of self-criticism and areas that clinicians can explore. To explore you can ask: "When was the first time you became aware of being self-critical? What was happening? What was the frustration, disappointment or dashed hope/dream/goal? Why was that hope/dream/goal of importance to you?" In other words, you are looking at the threats that were around when self-criticism started.

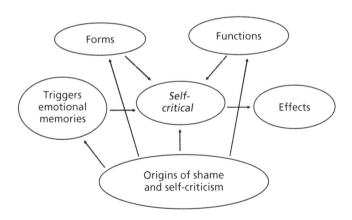

Figure 7 Self-criticism: a self-critical mind is also a threat-focused mind

Self-criticism can typically kick in when involved in situations linked to the original threat. For example, John's teacher could be very contemptuous and shaming of his poor English and told him he was lazy and would struggle in life because he was not very bright—only hard work would get him anywhere. John would feel "terrible heart sink" at these accusations. To avoid such shame feelings John did work harder. Later in life he became something of a workaholic to prove that he was "up to it" and to avoid those "isolating, heart sink" and "being no-good" feelings. When he had to write reports, if people were mildly critical of them this would reactivate the shame memories, of anger, self-criticism and feelings of being alone (recall that shame usually comes with feelings of being alone). He would then be highly self-critical. This was partly linked to hearing the voice of the teacher and partly out of panic, "Oh God, now what have I done!" So it's useful to link early threats with the origins and memories of self-criticism and possible triggers. John also believed that he needed to stay self-critical to keep himself working hard and not be a failure.

In our own work we found that there are different forms and functions of self-criticism (Gilbert, Clarke, Kempel, Miles, & Irons, 2004a). Attention to form is important. Whelton and Greenberg (2005) showed that it was not the cognitive content of self-criticism as much as the emotions of anger and contempt that were important in the pathogenic effects of self-criticism. One form we identified focuses on feeling inadequate. This type of self-criticism is usually about disappointment and feeling inferior. However, there is another form that is linked to hatred of the self. These are quite different and should be distinguished in your therapy. Self-hating tends to be low in nonclinical populations but high(er) in populations who come from difficult backgrounds. We suspect that self-hating is linked to a more abusive past but have no clear evidence as yet (see Andrews, 1998).

Self-hating can be directed at parts of the self such as one's body ("I hate my fat shape" or "I hate these feelings in me). So, when exploring self-criticism ask, "How does the critical part of you typically feel about you; what emotions does it direct at you?" I have to say that some current scales that supposedly measure self-criticism don't do so; they are more likely to measure things like social comparison or low self-esteem. One needs to think of self-criticism very much in terms of critical comments, dialogues and feelings within the self.

People can hate things about themselves but not necessarily blame themselves or feel responsible, e.g., for their looks or a birth mark or disfigurement, or lacking talent. So, issues of causality, blaming and disliking need to be distinguished. Note also that when people dislike things about themselves they can also be envious of others (Gilbert, 1992, pp. 246–252).

It can sometimes be useful to ask people to *imagine* their self-criticism. Ask, "If you could take your self-critic out of your head and look at it, what does it appear as (e.g., human or nonhuman)? What facial expressions does it have (assuming it has a face)? What emotions is it directing at you? What is its greatest fear/threat?" To understand the critic you can engage in chair work, putting the critic in a specific chair and exploring its thoughts and feelings. You can then move the person to a facing chair and explore ways of engaging with the critic. This Gestalt therapeutic intervention was further developed and popularized by Leslie Greenberg (e.g., see Whelton & Greenberg, 2005). When working with the self-critic you can develop a compassionate self first and then teach compassion for the critic (see Point 22). It is engaging with the narratives, meanings and emotions of self-criticism, not just the thoughts, that is central. For example, if a person imagines their self-critic as an angry, dominant person, you can ask them what would happen if they went to their inner critic (angry-dominant) with alternative and more rational thoughts. The client quickly gets insight that such would be dismissed and why cognitive interventions can run aground. This is why it's important to build up a part of the self that feels strong enough, and containing enough, to be able to work with a self-critical side (see Point 21).

95

Functional analysis

Functional analysis of self-criticism is very important. Sometimes there is no particular function—people just get angry with themselves when they make mistakes (e.g., dropping the ball in a ball game or forgetting something they had to do). However, you can look at how self-criticism guides a person by asking, "What would be your greatest fear in giving up self-criticism?" Typically you will find people fear becoming arrogant, lazy or uncontrolled. So, people may see self-criticism as having a range of *functions*, like making sure they pay attention to errors and to prevent them making errors in the future, to keep them on their toes. Self-criticism can act as a warning (e.g., if you don't lose weight nobody will like you). Therefore we teach how compassion offers a different way (is rooted in a different emotional system) for self-correction and improvement (see Point 13).

The German philosopher Friedrich Nietzsche said, "no one blames themselves without a secret wish for vengeance". Freud borrowed this for his theory of depression and thought that anger at oneself is really internalized anger towards others one is dependent on or ambivalent about: you are frightened of being angry with them so you take it out on yourself (Ellenberger, 1970). There is evidence that some people do experience rage but are fearful of it and inhibit their anger (Gilbert, Gilbert, & Irons, 2004b). So it is always worth exploring this possibility—to see if serious self-criticism and self-hatred are linked to unprocessed and feared hostile feelings towards others. The moment someone tells me "I'm not an angry person" I get suspicious. Occasionally it is true, but commonly this is a pointer to unprocessed and feared emotion. Commonly, people like to see themselves as "nice caring people" where anger is not part of that identity. We all have a capacity of anger—it's how we recognize it and work with it that is the issue. I have come across many chronically depressed people who, when they begin to work with and acknowledge their rage, without being ashamed and frightened of it, recover. If rage is experienced as frightening or shameful and not acknowledged as part of a repertoire of possible feelings, people can stay ashamed and frightened of it— thus maintaining a sense of impotent rage and powerlessness, and shame of feelings.

Self-monitoring and self-blame as safety strategies

CFT sees self-criticism in terms of safety strategies, with complex forms and functions that require exploring. One of these is power. As I've noted a number of times (e.g., Gilbert, 2007a, 2009a; Gilbert & Irons, 2005), people in religious contexts will blame themselves rather than their gods for setbacks and misfortunes. "What did we do to upset you, God of the Land, that you sent the famines?" History is full of self-deprecation and efforts to appease and sacrifice to powerful gods because we are frightened of them. Indeed, the concept of sin itself is a blaming process.

The link between self-criticism and powerful others, which Freud touched on, is particularly true in the case of self-criticism that arises in the context of abuse or trauma. This is because trauma, when perpetrated by powerful others, can automatically turn the victim to self-monitoring and self-regulating. So, we can also explore the responses and defences of the self-protection system and how that gets entangled with self-criticism. Consider that the first task of a child is to keep safe and stay out of trouble. If a parent's or bully's behaviour is unpredictable, it is like creeping around a sleeping tiger; you might be cross with yourself if you step on a twig that makes a sound that could wake the tiger to attack you. So, one must attend to one's own behaviour and self-monitor very carefully not to stir up the (tiger) bully and keep out of his/her way. This is how the self-monitoring and self-blaming system gets linked to aversive outcomes. Because one's own behaviour is *the only* possible source of control/protection (you can't change the bully), self-blame inevitably follows from doing things that (seem to) trigger the bully's aggression/rejection.

CFT spends time with clients explaining these *classical conditioning* models, and the functional value of self-monitoring and self-blame. The more of a framework clients have for understanding their self-criticism—as linked to safety strategies, the more reflective they can be and the more collaborative in engaging with these memories and developing self-compassion. Moreover, it helps people to understand why they "feel" (from the amygdala) to blame even through they logically (cortex) know they are not. There is a mismatch between two different systems. The amygdala does not listen to logic very much. I have found clients feel de-shamed by this explanation, e.g., "well it makes perfect sense because your amygdala and threat system cares only about keeping you safe and therefore it will self-monitor and self-blame as ways to do that (sleeping tiger example). So your feelings are about safety strategies not about the person you actually are".

In working with these memories we would first engage in developing the compassionate self that is able to be "wise, kind and parent-like" (see Point 21). When the client feels this part of them has been developed we might then explore re-engaging the memory which (say for Sara, see pages 88–92) might involve crouching and then gradually standing, focusing on the "then and now" differences; re-scripting, assertive work with "mother" in imagery or with an empty chair, or expressing her feelings in a letter (that may not be sent); or explore rage expression to desensitize to the "fear of rage". In other words, we are acting against the submissive–fearful strategy, and engaging in a more dominant self-protective strategy. Compassion or forgiveness to mother would come much later.

Note, too, that you can discuss with your client what the key elements are that they want to talk about and work on. For example, it might be to work with a sense of powerlessness and so sessions of assertive body-work could be helpful. Or it might be a sense of aloneness and therefore focusing on experiencing the therapist in that moment might be helpful; or it might be a sense of entrapment so the person may practice being assertive and then leaving the room; or it might be a sense of betrayal as in wanting to "get rid of the parent or break contact with the parent". One needs to break down the key issues and work on them individually. As with other therapies various forms of imagery re-scripting can be helpful (Lee, 2005; Wheatley et al., 2007).

The client collaborates to see what feels helpful and/or soothing and what does not. Because the client understands the three circles model then, like Yoga or physiotherapy, the client and therapist work together to try different things to bring the soothing system on line. The "bringing forth" of compassion is the explicit goal of the therapy and the client understands this, and of course one never goes further or more intensely than the person feels okay with.

Another key element of trauma and high levels of stress is that they can set up conflicting defences. For example, to a shame event one might feel angry, want to run away, and sad all at the same time. Because multiple emotions and defensive action tendencies can be aroused to the same event, some people become highly disorganized in affect regulation. Sara, for example (see pages 88–92, could have a lot of anger at herself and could be self-harming to try to manage her anger. She often suffered from a loss of drive. Feelings of self-soothing and connectedness to others were almost nonexistent. At times she would go into high arrested anger states, sitting in the chair in therapy hardly able to speak but the room would feel like a volcano of anger. Inside her, however, she would just ruminate on escape, "Why don't I just kill myself and get it over with—what am I doing here?" In the system I have outlined, her threat system was bouncing from arrested anger to arrested flight (Gilbert, 2007a; Gilbert et al., 2004b). The amygdala can generate a number of conflicting defences—rage attacks vs. fearful escape vs. submissive withdrawal vs. tearful care-eliciting. To act on one, the others are suppressed (see Dixon, 1998, for an animal model of conflicts of defences).

Distinguishing shame, guilt and humiliation: Responsibility vs. self-critical blaming

It is important to clarify the distinctions between different types of self-conscious emotion (Tracy et al., 2007). There are three major forms that are especially important: shame, guilt and humiliation. Shame and humiliation are very much to do with self and defending the self (see Figure 5) whereas guilt is about one's behaviour, awareness of harm to the other, and motivated desires to repair harm (Gilbert, 2007c, 2009a, 2009b; Tangney & Dearing, 2002). As a rough guide, keep in mind that shame, humiliation and guilt will each have a different attention focus, a different way of thinking and different behaviours. As a rough guide see Table 1.

Generally speaking, while shamelessness is not desirable, and like other emotions we need to learn how to face it and tolerate it, evidence suggests that shame and humiliation feelings (which are about feeling attacked or vulnerable in some way) are often unhelpful and can lead to destructive, defensive behaviours (Tangney & Dearing, 2002). In contrast, guilt is an emotion of behavioural responsibility, including responsibility to make amends. Consider two men who have had affairs and their wives discover them. A shame-focused response would be thinking about how bad one was and that other people would turn against him, and that he needs to make amends so that other people will like him again. Shame is (bad) "me, me, me". A humiliation response would be to become angry and (say) blame his wife for not being attractive enough such that he needed to have affairs, or be angry with the person who revealed his secret. Other responses might be denial or minimization and so forth. A

Table 1 Rule of thumb distinctions between shame, humiliation and guilt

Internal shame rank mentality	Humiliation rank mentality	Guilt care mentality
Inwardly directed attention on damage to self and reputation	Externally directed attention is the threat or damage done to the self by the other	Externally directed attention on hurt caused with empathy for the other
Feelings of anxiety paralysis, heart-sinking, confusion, emptiness, self-directed anger	Feelings of anger, injustice, vengeance	Feelings of sorrow, sadness and remorse
Thoughts focused on negative judgements of the "whole self"	Thoughts focused on unfairness of any negative judgements or behaviours of others	Thoughts focused on the "harm to the other", sympathy and empathy
Behaviours focused on submissive-appeasing, wanting to be liked again, or closing down and moving away, avoidance, displacement, denial, self-harm	Behaviours focused on vengeance and silencing the other—having power over the other, belittling and humiliating back	Behaviours focused on trying to repair harm, offering genuine apologies, making amends for the benefit of others

guilt response, however, would be a recognition of the betrayal, the harm done, genuine concern for the upset he's caused his wife, with a genuine desire to help his wife feel better and repair the damage.

Sometimes if people have been unkind or harmful to others it is important to change their shame (bad me) based experiences to guilt (harm awareness) based ones, that is to help them tolerate aversive feelings when they do hurtful things, without it becoming (just) an attack on the self. Sometimes, to be able to process the harm they do to others, they must first process the harm that was done to them.

There are also disorders that look like problems of over-responsibility, as occurs in obsessional compulsive disorder (OCD) or excessive caring (Wroe & Salkovskis, 2000). It is unclear, however, how much OCD people feel *personally bad* and are focused on "a bad self" rather than genuine concern for "the other" but it does seem as if some experience "guilt attacks", which are not so different from panic attacks.

So, as a rule of thumb you can look at where people are allocating their attention, what they are focused on in their thoughts and ruminations, and what they want to do. Keep in mind these *are not mutually exclusive*, and various blends of each can ebb and flow in therapy and in general.

It is important, then, that people learn to understand guilt, not turn harmful acts into self-focused shame or just become angry if somebody stimulates this in them. Guilt is helpful to building relationships in a way that shame is not (Baumeister, Stillwell, & Heatherton, 1994). Guilt is something we must think about and tolerate. While there is much discussion on tolerating sadness, anxiety and anger there is very little research on learning to tolerate guilt and how to behave appropriately—but this is important in CFT. Guilt can be normal and natural and is to be expected because no one can go through life without being hurtful, damaging and plain unkind.

Distinguishing compassionate self-correction from shame-based self-attacking

When working with self-shame and self-criticism (and shame vs. guilt) it is useful to distinguish two different emotion systems underpinning self-correction. For example, if you ask people to completely give up self-criticism they often worry that they will become arrogant or lazy or uncontrolled. This is true, even of therapists in a workshop! However, as noted above, if I ask you to imagine the part of you that is critical, to see it looking back at you as it were, and what emotions it is directing at you, the chances are these emotions will be ones of frustration, anger, contempt or disappointment. *These are all emotions of the threat system*. Therefore, our self-criticism of this type stimulates the threat system. It is not focused on our well-being.

The key, then, is to align with a different motivational system for orientating us towards self-correction. This comes when we realise that we would actually *like* to do a good job, e.g., to treat our clients well and see them improve. In other words, we are positively motivated to be at our best once we learn to stimulate that motivational system. So, CFT builds on other cognitive and positive psychology principles of focusing on our strengths. This approach has become increasingly important in the cognitive-behavioural psychotherapies (Synder & Ingram, 2006). In this spirit we focus on the three circles model, helping people to contrast the distinction between compassionate self-improvement and shame/fear-based self-criticism. This is outlined in Table 2.

Again, this is fairlystraight forward. Imagine a child who is struggling at school with one of two teachers. The first is very

Table 2 Distinguishing compassionate self-correction from shame-based self-criticism and attacking

Compassionate self-correction:	Shame-based self-attacking:
• Focuses on the desire to improve	• Focuses on the desire to condemn and punish
• Focuses on growth and enhancement	• Focuses on punishing past errors
• Is forward-looking	• Is often backward looking
• Is given with encouragement, support and kindness	• Is given with anger, frustration, contempt, disappointment
• Builds on positives (e.g., seeing what one did well and then considering learning points)	• Focuses on deficits and fear of exposure
• Focuses on attributes and specific qualities of self	• Focuses on a global sense of self
• Focuses on and hopes for success	• Focuses on high fear of failure
• Increases chances of engaging	• Increases chances of avoidance and withdrawal
For transgression/mistakes:	For transgression/mistakes:
• Guilt, engage with	• Shame, avoidance, fear
• Sorrow, remorse	• Heart-sink, lowered mood
• Reparation	• Aggression
• Use the example of the encouraging supportive teacher with the child who is struggling	• Use the example of the critical teacher with the child who is struggling

Adapted from Gilbert, P. (2009a) *The Compassionate Mind*. London: Constable & Robinson and Oaklands, CA: New Harbinger.

good at spotting errors and is quite critical and maybe slightly frustrated with the child's mistakes. He or she believes that it is necessary to keep children on their toes otherwise, without a degree of fear, they will be lazy. In contrast, the second teacher has concerns for the well-being of the child, and is able to encourage the child to *accept and learn from their mistakes* in a compassionate way. Which teacher would you prefer to teach your child? In his passionately written book *How Children Fail* John Holt (1990) argued that much of Western education teaches us to be frightened of our mistakes. Therapists may thus be working hard against the social grain.

Another way that you can help people recognize the harm of self-criticism (recall that you can elicit images of people's own self-criticism) is to explore the origins of self-criticism. Commonly, it will be the voice of a parent or teacher and you can ask, "Did those individuals criticize you out of a *genuine* care for your well-being? Did you feel care for you when criticized (or more likely anger)? Did they have your best interests at heart? Does your self-critical side have your best interests at heart or is it just rather angry and disappointed?" You might also ask, "If you have your best interests at heart how would you *really like* to talk to yourself? How would you help somebody you really cared about see this issue? How would you help a child?" In these examples you are helping people recognize that they probably would not be harshly critical to others, that self-criticism doesn't really serve their best interests, whereas compassionate self-correction does. Of course, they'll think critical things of other people at times, but it is recognizing that they still would not voice them because they see that would be harmful not helpful. So, it's not the correction and the awareness of errors that is the key *but it's the emotions that we bring to the process of trying to improve.*

Working with self-criticism

Because self-criticism is a complex process, often associated with self-identity and safety behaviours/strategies, we do not try to dismantle it head on. Rather, we are likely to say to clients, "Feel free to maintain your self-criticism if you find it helpful. However, we are going to teach new ways to think about and treat yourself including compassionate self-correction. You may find, as you practice these, that they serve you better than self-criticism." Trying to work with self-criticism simply by looking at the evidence for and against rarely works in high-self-criticism and shame clients. Once clients don't feel under any threat to "change or get rid of safety strategies" until they have new strategies, they feel more confident at trying things.

14

Threat and the compensations of achievement

While shame can typically lead to the safety strategies of self-criticism, avoidance, closing down, hiding and various unhelpful ways of trying to regulate emotions, shame can also lead to invigorated drive behaviours in the form of achievement seeking—linked to the "musts" and "have tos"—as in Rational Emotive Behaviour Therapy (REBT; Dryden, 2009). Alfred Adler (1870–1937) argued that people who feel inferior (have an inferiority complex) may strive to *compensate* and prove themselves to others—a view now well accepted by most psychotherapies. CFT therefore links to the research on compensation and achievement. Some years ago, McClelland, Atkinson, Clark and Lowell (1953) made a distinction in motivation theory between value achievers and need achievers. Value achievers set their achievements to bring pleasures and stretch themselves, whereas need achievers set their standards to try to impress others. These themes have been taken up by other researchers. For example, Dykman (1998) suggested that there are two main motivations behind achievement, which he called *growth* seeking versus *validation* seeking. Growth seekers enjoy challenges and their ability to learn and mature through challenges/mistakes. Validation seekers, however, feel under constant pressure to prove themselves as likeable and acceptable to others. He also suggested that validation seeking is a defensive coping strategy that develops in the context of critical and perfectionist parenting. In a series of studies Dunkley and colleagues (e.g., Dunkley, Zuroff, & Blankstein, 2006) explored various measures of perfectionism and suggested two underlying factors: the first is setting and striving for personal

109

standards; the second is striving to avoid criticism/rejection from others—labelled "evaluative concerns". Dunkley et al. (2006) found that it is the evaluative concerns dimension that is linked to various psychopathological indicators. Our research has also shown that *insecure* striving, to avoid inferiority (which is different from seeking superiority) can be distinguished from *secure* non-striving. Insecure striving is to avoid the *social* consequences of rejection, exclusion and shame (Gilbert et al., 2007). Secure non-strivers think they are accepted whether they succeed or fail.

Goss and Gilbert (2002) suggested that this was particularly true of people with eating disorders. Anorexic people focus on feelings of pride in their control of their weight and impulses to eat. When they lose control of their weight or impulses to eat this activates high threat and alarm. For these individuals it is the drive system that they are using to try to regulate the threat system. Figure 8, which Ken Goss and I developed to depict eating-disorder problems, offers a simplistic view of this.

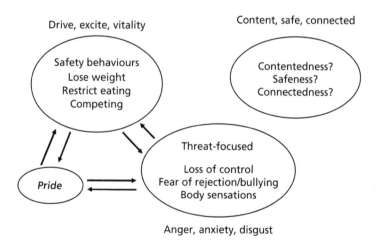

Figure 8 Types of affect regulator systems (developed with Ken Goss, 2009)

We can leave out the arrows linking the contentment and soothing system because we don't know how they actually work in these cases. This is a model that can be used for a whole range of individuals who have become competitive and striving in order to stave off feelings of threat or to feel connected. This is an increasing problem in our Western society (Gilbert, 2009a; Pani, 2000) and may be one of the reasons why we have growing problems with adolescent depression, anxiety, drug taking and self-harm (Twenge et al., 2010). When you talk to these adolescents the sense of disconnectedness (especially from adult society), inferiority, aloneness and the struggle they have to really feel valued by others is sad. Schools, businesses and Western governments over the last 20 years have deliberately infected our societies with beliefs that only the competitive and able can make good—we must all have a "competitive edge" and prove ourselves in the market. It is problematic because it affects our brains (Pani, 2000) and creates high levels of inequality that are known to be pathogenic and unhelpful to our well-being (Wilkinson & Pickett, 2009).

If you draw out the three circles for your clients, and explain this to them, they very quickly see what's happening and why. As to whether they will then form a contract with you, to try to balance their systems by becoming more compassionate and soothing, that is another matter. They will often hold strong beliefs that only if they are successful will people like them—one client told me that she had been told, "Those who come second are the first losers", and "No one remembers who came second". So, it is useful to distinguish value-based achievement striving from threat-based attachment striving—the latter being strongly linked to shame proneness and fears of social exclusion and rejection. There can also be a fear of positive emotions associated with contentment and affiliation (see Point 29), and striving can be built into the sense of self-identity. You can use behavioural experiments, planning non-achievement fun things, playfulness and desensitization to positive effect, and help people think about their striving in different ways.

111

What emerges from this research on achievement motivation is that problems in people's ability to feel connected to others, able to rely on them and feel safe with them, generate desires for them to try to "earn their place". In doing this they become over reliant on the incentive-seeking dopaminergic system to give them a sense of positive feelings and self-security. Indeed, people who become perfectionists, high striving or feel they need to prove themselves will often only get temporary relief if they do succeed. The other thing that strikes you when working with some perfectionist strivers, and those desperately wanting to prove themselves, is that they will often talk about having this feeling of "being alone"—not really connected to others, not feeling a sense of belonging. They may also struggle to feel happy and contented states of intimacy and closeness to others. These are feelings that we discussed above in relationship to shame and it is important to explore them because they may become a focus for therapy, linked to the problem in activating the connectedness and soothing systems.

Self-focused vs. compassionate goals

Crocker and Canevello (2008) explored two types of self-image goals. One was compassionate, wanting to help others. Concerns with altruistic goals, with wanting to help others, have been observed in very young children (Warneken & Tomasello, 2009). The other goal was self-focused, wanting to achieve and create good impressions on others. We see here similarities with value versus need achievers, growth versus validation seekers, and the motives of getting along versus getting ahead. However, importantly, compassion goals were associated with feelings of closeness, connectedness and social support and inversely related to conflict, loneliness and being afraid and confused by feelings. In contrast, self-focused goals showed the reverse relationships. Reed and Aquino (2003) suggested that caring, kindness and honesty attributes can become important for a self-identity, which they call a moral identity. *Wanting* to be a kind and compassionate person (i.e., harness the care-giving mentality for self and social role co-creation) contributes to more benevolent behaviours and values—especially to outgroups. So, self-identity imagery goals, the kind of self one wants to be, tries to be, and practises to be, have important effects on social behaviour and well-being. This research should be kept in mind when we look at developing the compassionate self (Points 21–29).

Doing and achieving

It is incorrect to see CFT as only concerned with one (soothing) system. The main focus of CFT is a *balancing* of the three affect systems *not just stimulating the soothing system*. Sometimes it is important to work on the drive and achieving system as well, by shifting *threat*-based achieving to *value* achieving. "Doing" is very important in behavioural activation approaches to depression (Gilbert, 2009b; Martell, Addis, & Jacobson, 2001). Nor is CFT the end of ambition. The Dalai Lama travels the world trying to promote compassion; in ACT, committing oneself to the values and goals is key to personal growth and development.

Compassionate behaviour can also involve providing people with things that are important for their flourishing in life. For example, at Christmas time, providing a child with a long-wanted bicycle so that he or she can be like his or her friends could be an act of compassion. If we have a self-deprivation psychology then learning how to enjoy and provide for ourselves can be important. Learning to take joy from our and other people's achievements is also important for balancing our emotions. However, as in other therapies, there is a distinction between taking joy in having and "feeling a need and must have" (Dryden, 2009).

Part 2

COMPASSION PRACTICE

Understanding soothing: The wider context of balancing affect-regulation systems

Soothing and balancing our emotions is related to compassion (Point 16) but should be seen as a complex and multi-component process. Here are some key aspects:

(Skilled) affection and kindness

As outlined above, a powerful way of soothing is via physical contact, kindness and warmth. Feeling that the other person genuinely cares about you and is able to provide caring is soothing. Kindness, however, often has to be supplemented with other qualities such as skill and abilities. You are more likely to be reassured by your doctor if you know he/she is highly competent, knowledgeable or wise. You are more likely to feel reassured if you know the "other person" understands you. This issue of "holding such authority" for the client is important in therapy.

Social referencing

A child may be anxious about approaching a threatening or novel stimulus and looks to the parent to see how they are feeling about the stimulus. The parent displays interest and approaches the stimulus, or may interact with the stimulus in a positive way. They may encourage the child to explore the stimulus. Thus, reassurance here arises from social referencing and modelling. A more complex example is when a person is able to socially reference their own feelings and discovers that others have the same types of feelings as they do and are not alarmed or shamed by them. This is a major compassion process in group therapies (Bates, 2005).

A more complex form of social referencing is what the compassion theorist Neff (2003a) calls "common humanity". Here we recognize that our fantasies, fears, worries and depressions don't make us abnormal but we share them as part of the human condition—others are like us too.

Living in the mind of others

Our abilities to feel safe in the social world often come from how we feel or think others feel and think about us (see Gilbert, 1992, Chapter 7, 2007a, Chapter 5). When we interact with others, so that they show pleasure in our presentations and liking, then we can feel safe. In fact, people spend much of their time thinking about other people's feelings towards them, have special cognitive systems for thinking about what others are thinking (called theory of mind) and many of our goals are orientated to try to earn other people's approval and respect, and be accepted in groups. Over 100 years ago the social psychologist Charles Cooley referred to this as the *Looking Glass Self* (Cooley, 1902/1922). Unlike Freud, Cooley focused on the power of the social group and social relationships to shape our minds and regulate our emotions. It is unfortunate that this social approach to our states of mind got lost in the more individualistic and medicalized therapies that subsequently emerged. Cooley still has much to teach us.

In CFT the minds of others, and our experiences and thoughts about them, is crucial to our emotion-regulation abilities—and for good evolutionary reasons (Gilbert, 2007c). If you think about how you would like your lovers, close friends, counselling peers, clients and bosses to see you—it will mainly be to value you and see you as desirable, helpful, talented and able. If you can create these feelings in the mind of others then three things happen. First, the world is *safe* and you can know others will not attack or reject you because they value you. Second, you will be able to co-create meaningful roles for mutual support, sexual relationships and sharing. Third, receiving signals that others are valuing and caring of you has direct effects on your physiology and soothing system. Many clients can be frightened of how they live in the mind of others and that others may view them as odd, weak, inadequate or bad. Working with these internal representations of "how one exists in your mind" can be experienced as soothing.

Being heard and understood

People can feel threatened and become defensive when they think that others do not understand them and/or have little interest in "hearing them" or taking their point of view into serious account. We can feel soothed when we feel the opposite—that others see our views as something to be paid attention to, articulate and *valid* and—importantly—not to be overridden or dismissed. This need can take precedence over more physical acts of soothing. For example, a client became upset and tearful. To prevent this her husband would often try to sooth her by putting his arm around her. He felt hurt when she tried to push him away. Her account was that she felt he was saying "there, there" and trying to quieten her feelings rather than actively listening to her concerns and giving her a chance to express herself and be understood. For her, to have someone *really listen*, and be with her in her distress, and tolerate that distress was soothing. Sometimes people cry when they are angry and want to be heard and not comforted!

Empathic validation

This involves the experience that another mind/person *understands* our mind—our feelings, thoughts and points of view— and validates them. Thus, a therapist might say to a grieving woman, "Losing your husband like that must have been a horrible experience for you; your feelings make a lot of sense because . . .". Empathic validation means that: (1) we have understanding of the other person's point of view and connect to it because we can connect to our own basic human psychology—the other person is not an unfathomable alien; and (2) validation means that we validate their lived experience as genuine, and that it makes sense as part of the human condition and their personal lives. Thus, empathic validation is more than reflection (e.g., "You feel sad or angry about this"), but acknowledges a client's reaction as an understandable and valid experience (e.g., "Given X or Y . . . it is understandable that you would feel . . ."). Once again, however, empathic validation begins via our experience of how we exist in the mind of others. *In*validation can be: "This is neurotic; you have no need to feel like this; you shouldn't feel this; you are being irrational, etc." Many conflicts can arise when people feel others are invalidating them through lack of interest or efforts to understand or care, or are pathologizing them or are trying to "make" them change.

Many people have a complex mixture of feelings that may be difficult to understand and of which they may be fearful (Leahy, 2002, 2005). They may cope with these via avoidance, denial, dissociation or by replacing one feeling with another. Social referencing, being listened to and empathic validation are important experiences of "what is going on in the mind of the other" that help a person come to terms with, and understand, their own feelings. Client and therapist work together on the "basic feeling issues" and help the person be aware of and address emotional memories, unmet needs or key fears that might make feelings frightening (see Gilbert & Leahy, 2007). It is also useful to draw out and list the various complex feelings that can emerge in any one experience.

Reasoning

CBT puts a lot of emphasis on reasoning and "testing out beliefs". When we feel threatened the attention narrows down onto the threat and we shift to "better safe than sorry" thinking (Gilbert, 1998). We can feel soothed when we are able to stand back and examine our thoughts in detail and come to a different perspective. As children we can learn how to reason by observing others (e.g., parents and teachers), adopting their explanations, values and styles of reasoning to be in line with their values, and via direct instructions on how to think about this or that. CBT therapists help people with these processes of thinking and reasoning in the face of strong emotions or fears. Thus, the degree of change may be how far the therapist can enable a person to look more deeply at their reasoning, stand back, take a view from the balcony, and *experiment* with alternative views and behaviours. Processes that help us de-escalate threats or cope in new ways can affect soothing and reassurance. So, reasoning is obviously very helpful and important to how safe or threatened in the world we feel. Keep in mind, though, that people need to be able to *feel* reassured by their alternative thoughts and that there are various reasons why these feelings may be problematic.

Insight

We can feel relieved when we come to have insight into how things work and are connected. Insight is linked to our abilities to stand back and refocus our thoughts—without insight of why this is useful, such efforts may just be "following the advice of the therapist". Insight, though, is also an emotional experiential process. In Buddhism, for example, years of meditation practice can gives rise to *insight* (as direct experience) into the illusions of the self—which enables people to find inner peace and compassion.

Ruminating

There is now much evidence that ruminating can be highly detrimental to mental health (see pages 63–66). This, in CFT terms, is partly because it continues to (over) activate the threat self-protection systems. So, all therapies (such as mindfulness) that help to lower rumination by redirecting attention can be helpful. Compassion refocusing can be especially useful to help people switch out of threat-focused ruminating cycles.

Desensitization

Key to many behavioural approaches are those linked to forms of exposure and desensitization. In some cases, coming to feel safe requires that we are able to experience both internal and external fears in new ways. Thus, in CFT the ability to "stay with" and learn to *tolerate* frightening feelings or situations can be key to soothing. However, just as the child may use a parent to navigate these domains so may a client need to feel "held and contained" by the therapist during the process. An inability to trust others may be a key reason why people become resistant to engaging in these processes—because they feel they have no safe base. In fact, a key ingredient of successful behaviour therapy may be the way the therapist is able to encourage, hold and contain the anxieties of their clients as they engage in various exposures (Gilbert, 1989; Gilbert & Leahy, 2007). If they don't succeed in this the client may simply drop out.

What is less well articulated in behaviour therapy is the recognition of just how frightened some people are of a whole range of *positive* emotions and outcomes—especially those of affection—and then the need to desensitize people to be able to feel and tolerate positive emotions. It has long been thought that positive emotions/events, by definition, are always felt positively—but they are not (see Point 29).

Developing courage

CFT puts a lot of store on the development of courage, because we often ask people to face things and feel things that are unpleasant or frightening. Those with traumatic memories will need to learn how to face them and re-script them. Courage is more likely to develop if we have a sense of support and *en*couragement. Compassionate courage helps us tolerate and cope with difficult feelings. Distress tolerance, then, is about developing courage. Indeed, without at least some courage it may be very difficult to put compassion into action (Gilbert, 2009a).

Overview

There are many other processes that can help to settle the threat systems and engage soothing (e.g., mindfulness). Shortly we will look at forms of compassionate attention, compassionate thinking, compassionate behaviour, compassionate motivation and compassionate feeling as ways to balance our motivations and affect-regulation systems. The full and active presence of the therapist is key rather than a detached, technical, behind-the-couch or over-controlling therapeutic persona. CFT, thus, is not to be confused with just being "nice" to people or with "love" (Gilbert & Leahy, 2007).

16

The nature of compassion

Compassion is linked to various traits such as warmth and agreeableness (see Point 7) and its development from childhood is strongly linked to early affectionate experiences and attachment security (Gillath, Shaver, & Mikulincer, 2005). Compassion itself can be defined in many ways (see Point 1). The Dalai Lama defines compassion as a sensitivity to the suffering of self and others, with a deep commitment to try to relieve it. In Mahayana Buddhism, mindfulness creates the conditions for a calm mind and compassion for a transformed mind. Each works together like the wings of a bird. The Buddha understood the transformative processes of compassion and recognized that we needed to train our minds in many different ways. He talked about the eight-fold path as a path for compassion and insight:

- *Right view*: develop clear insight into the true causes of suffering as being linked to attachments and craving.
- *Right concentration*: related to focused attention such as on mindfulness and compassion.
- *Right intention*: linked to the motivation to be caring–compassionate.
- *Right speech*: linked to interpersonal relating, saying kind rather than hurtful things.
- *Right action*: linked to behaviour that tries to heal rather than destroy.
- *Right livelihood*: linked to choice of career and how one conducts oneself at work.
- *Right efforts*: linked to the need to practise with effort/dedication.
- *Right mindfulness*: linked to paying attention "in the moment" in a compassionate way.

Threat mind vs. compassionate mind

You might consider how if our threat-protection system is active, so that we have "threat mind", this will influence our feelings and motives, what we attend to, what we think about and how we think about it, and our behaviour. The kinds of images and fantasies that pop into one's head, and our (day) dreams, may also have threat themes. So, when we are in "threat mind" all these will be quite different from when we are trying to generate a compassionate mind (see Figure 9—something you can draw for your clients).

In contrast, a compassionate mind can organize our minds in different ways. So, compassionate attention, compassionate thinking, compassionate behaviours, compassionate feelings, compassionate motives and compassionate imagery and fantasies are quite different from threat-focused ones. Helping clients understand these distinctions, between threat mind and compassionate mind, in these relatively simple ways can be helpful to them. Part of one's work is helping people recognize when they are shifting into threat mind, and ruminating in threat mind. So, you teach them how to pay attention to any shift in attentional focus, in bodily feelings, thoughts and urges to action, and then to make deliberate efforts to refocus and activate compassionate mind. Clearly a whole range of interventions from CBT, ACT and DBT can be helpful in achieving this.

Keep in mind, too, that these mind states are not just reactive. Sometimes we can just wake up in the morning in a mild threat-mind pattern, feeling mildly anxious, irritable, fed up, tired or depressed. These different brain states are clearly related to different systems in our brains. If we have been under stress recently or suffered setbacks and losses, the threshold for shifting into threat mind can be significantly lowered and we find ourselves becoming upset over quite small things. Again, it's useful to explain this to people as a natural, normal consequence of stress—but one that we need to be alert to and practice focusing instead on compassion.

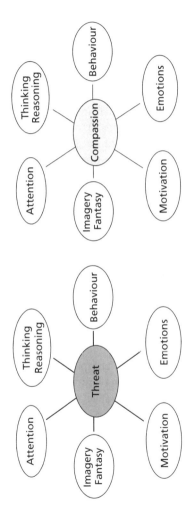

Figure 9 A comparison of threatened and compassionate mentalities. Reproduced with kind permission from Gilbert, P. (2009b) *Overcoming Depression*, 3rd edn. London: Constable & Robinson and New York: Basic Books

A more complex view

CFT is based on an evolutionary-neuroscience approach, which views our capacity for compassion as having evolved out of our capacity for *altruism and caring* behaviour (Gilbert, 1989, 2005a). Altruism makes possible a desire to help others reach their goals and alleviate suffering. Children as young as 14–18 months have an innate interest in helping others reach their goals—irrespective of rewards (Warneken & Tomasello, 2009). With regard to caring, CFT builds from Fogel, Melson and Mistry's (1986) model of nurturance (Gilbert, 1989). They defined the core elements of care-nurturance as: ". . . the provision of guidance, protection and care for the purpose of fostering developmental change congruent with the expected potential for change of the object of nurturance" (p. 55). They also suggest that nurturance involves *awareness* of the need to be nurturing, *motivation* to nurture, *expression* of nurturing feelings, *understanding* what is needed to be nurturing, and an ability to match nurturing with the *feedback* from the impact of nurturing on the other. Nurturing, then, needs to be skilfully enacted. Gilbert (2000a) argued that theses aspects can be self-directed as well as aimed at external targets. Nurturing is a core aspect of compassion and problems with any of these competencies can interfere with compassion in relationships—including therapeutic ones. So, compassion can involve a range of feelings, thoughts and behaviours, such as those aimed to nurture, look after, protect, rescue, teach, guide, mentor, soothe and offer feelings of acceptance and belonging—*in order to benefit the target of one's caring* (Gilbert, 1989, 2007a, 2007b).

Such interventions require a number of different *interdependent* competencies and attributes. To illuminate these interdependencies they can be represented as two interacting circles called the *compassion circles* (Gilbert, 2005a, 2009a). These interconnected elements enhance each other. All are infused with basic warmth (rather than, say, cold detachment).

We can distinguish, then, an inner circle of *attributes*—the "whats" of compassion and an outer circle of *skills*. The outer circle contains the "how tos" for the inner circle. So, we can learn to direct our attention compassionately, to think and reason compassionately, to feel compassionately, to behave compassionately, and to generate compassionate images and imaginings; to work on creating a bodily sense of compassion. Combined, attributes and skills constitute the compassionate mind.

Compassionate minds are something that we can choose to develop in our relationships with other people, compassionately focusing our attention, thoughts and behaviours. Important, too, is to develop the compassionate mind in our relationship with ourselves. When we train our minds for compassion, this is called *compassionate mind training* (CMT). The key aspects and attributes of compassion (inner ring) and the processes to develop them (outer ring) are displayed in Figure 10.

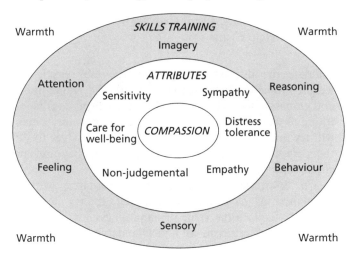

Figure 10 Multimodal compassionate mind training (CMT). Reproduced with kind permission from Gilbert, P. (2009a) *The Compassionate Mind*. London: Constable & Robinson and Oaklands, CA: New Harbinger

Space does not allow detailed description of all the attributes and skills (but see Gilbert, 2009a, pp. 194–210). However, a brief outline is given in Table 3.

Many CFT interventions use standard CBT interventions relating to: inference chaining; problem solving; working to reduce rumination; generating alternatives; looking at the evidence; developing acceptance; practicing graded exposure; utilizing behavioural experiments; and helping to reduce safety behaviours—to name just a few. These are very important skills that are not distinctive to CFT; it is the context and manner in which they are applied that is unique.

An example

Let's imagine that somebody has had a setback such as failing at a job interview, or has put on weight. They feel bad about themselves and are self-critical. Here are some procedures that we might use. Help clients to:

1 Validate the distress arising from the job rejection or weight problem. Help clients be sensitive to, validating of and empathic to their distress (but not self-pitying) before trying to work with it. This can be very important as many will try and dismiss it, minimize it, tell themselves to pull themselves together, or even be angry that they are "not coping and getting into a state".

2 Learn emotional tolerance and acceptance without avoidance or "fighting with myself to try to force control". Explore the value of mindfulness.

3 Recognize self-criticism as understandable but unhelpful; seeing *behind* the criticism *to the fears and sadnesses*. Then developing compassion for those.

4 Prepare themselves to engage with the inner distress or self-criticism with their soothing breathing rhythm (even just for a few seconds, see pages 141–142).

Table 3 Compassionate attributes and compassionate skills are used to counteract the feelings, styles of thinking and behaviour that arise when we are angry, anxious, depressed or distressed

Compassionate attributes	Compassionate skills
1 Developing a motivation to be caring towards self and others—reduce suffering and flourish. The "intentionality" and recognition of the value of the effort to develop compassion is crucial and often precedes "feelings" of compassion.	1 Learning to deliberately focus our attention on things that are helpful and bring a balanced perspective. This will involve "mindful awareness" and developing mindful attention—using our attention to bring to mind helpful compassionate images and/or a sense of self. However, this is not an avoidance tactic.
2 Developing sensitivity to feelings and needs of self and others (different from just being aware of vulnerability, fears or worries).	2 Learning to think and reason, objectively, looking at the evidence and bringing a balanced perspective. Standing back, writing down and reflecting on styles of thinking and reasoning.
3 Developing sympathy, being moved and emotionally in tune with feelings in self and others (in contrast to being dissociated, angry or fearful of our feelings). It also means being more sensitive to needs for growth, e.g., for help, or to take time out.	3 Learning to plan and engage in behaviours that act to relieve distress; and move us (and others) forward to our (or their) life goals—to flourish.
4 Developing abilities to tolerate rather than avoid difficult feelings, memories or situations (including positive emotions).	4 Compassionate behaviour often needs courage and taking action.
5 Developing insight and understanding of how our, or another, mind works, why we/they feel what we/they feel.	
6 Developing an accepting, non-condemning and non-submissive orientation to ourselves and others.	

Adapted from Gilbert, P. (2009a) *The Compassionate Mind*. London: Constable & Robinson and Oaklands, CA: New Harbinger

5 Refocus attention on what would be helpful and supportive in this situation, for example bringing to mind memories of previous successes or of people's support, or of the compassionate self (see Point 21) or of compassionate images (see Point 26)—help the client to think for themselves what would be helpful to attend to here.

6 Imagine the compassionate self dealing with this issue (e.g., rejection or weight problem).

7 Recognize (self-critical) rumination as understandable and a common process but recognize the value of refocusing on (say) becoming a compassionate self (see Point 21).

8 Imagine the compassionate self being compassionate to one's self-criticism and the fears and sadnesses that are often part of the self-criticism (see Point 23). Ask the client to engage in rumination for a few moments and then go through the "becoming a compassionate self exercise" and ask them to note the changes.

9 Explore how they would speak to a friend—but spend time enabling them to *feel* what they're saying rather than just attending to the content—in fact content is less important than motives and feelings here. So, again, becoming the compassionate self might be the best place to explore this.

10 Utilize various cognitive and compassionate concepts such as recognizing that one is not alone with these difficulties (common humanity), opening oneself to recognition that suffering is the human condition, depersonalizing, recognizing and counteracting black-and-white thinking, recognizing and counteracting overgeneralizations—while validating the understandable tendency to think like this when we feel threatened and distressed. However, in each case give plenty of space and time for the person to *feel* these counteracting cognitions as helpful; they should be practised with *an inner "kind" of voice*.

11 Engage with self-criticism using compassionate chair work (see Point 22).

12 Write a compassionate letter (see Point 27).

13 Think of what are the most supportive behaviours and actions to do in the short term and in the longer term.
14 Refocus using compassionate images. Imagine oneself in a dialogue or interaction with a compassionate image.

These are just a few ideas and we will explore some of them in more detail below.

Refining compassion attributes

When we move into compassionate focusing and imagery we will focus on four key qualities within the image: "*wisdom*, *strength*, *warmth/kindness* and *non-judgemental/condemning*", so definitions are in order and this can be shared with clients. However, we will also focus a lot on the issue of the inner circle so that people can develop and feel caring motives and be tolerant of distress, etc.

Wisdom

Compassion and wisdom are intimately linked and feed each other (Cozolino, 2008). Research on wisdom shows that it is associated with a range of mental-health benefits, maturity and prosocial behaviour (e.g., see Ardelt, 2003). Ardelt suggested that wisdom is a multi-faceted concept, linked to cognitive, reflective and affective components, that involves first a *motivation* to understand, "to know and learn" with an openness to the new; seeking knowledge rather than relying on tradition or superstition. Second, an ability to *reflect* on the human condition and human nature, and grapple with complexity and paradox (e.g., death, decay and suffering). In Buddhism it is seeing through the illusions "of self"; in evolutionary psychology it is recognizing how we are constructed (outside our choice) and that "we all just find ourselves here" (see Point 8). Third, *wise reasoning* enables us to think about situations from different points of view (as in CBT); to cultivate a calm mind (as in mindfulness), and minimize projection and emotional reasoning;

it is non-judging or condemning. Wisdom is how we learn from experience. Fourth, *emotions* underpinning wisdom are based on compassion and caring, to relieve suffering and promote prosperity of self and others. Wisdom is something that emerges over the life cycle and through experience. Psychotherapy, therefore, can be about supporting people in their search for wisdom—and in the end it is wisdom that helps them. Wise mind is a key focus in DBT (Linehan, 1993). Importantly, note here how much many of these qualities depend on first being able to mentalize one's own mental states (Bateman & Fonagy, 2006) and thus the development of mentalizing must underpin wisdom; indicating once again how overlapping many of these areas are.

While there are paths to wisdom there is also wisdom itself. Wisdom comes from insight, knowing and understanding. Wisdom transforms the mind.

Intuitive wisdom

CFT uses the concept of intuitive wisdom to help people connect with their own inner understanding and validate their feelings. For example, people often understand the three circle model—and we suggest this is because they have "intuitive wisdom". A client, who came from an abusive background but had worked with a therapist who only wanted to work in the here and now, left that therapy. Some time later she came to see me. She clearly needed (and wanted) to work on background and I refer to this as her intuitive wisdom—she knew what was necessary for her. Wherever possible CFT asks the client, "What is your intuitive wisdom on this issue?" This is the basis of collaboration. The language and focus of our approach is important. Of course, sometimes intuitive wisdom is not so wise!

Strength

One of the most common confusions in compassion is that people see it as weak or soft. However, as Sharon Salzberg (1995) put it:

Compassion is not at all weak. It is the strength that arises out of seeing the true nature of suffering in the world. Compassion allows us to bear witness to that suffering, whether it is in ourselves or others, without fear; it allows us to name injustice without hesitation, and to act strongly, with all the skill at our disposal. To develop this mind state of compassion, the second of the brahma-viharas, is to learn to live as the Buddha put it, with sympathy for all living beings, without exception.

(p. 103)

These are somewhat idealistic (e.g., it is not "without fear" but the ability to tolerate fear that is key)—but you can see the point. She goes on to make the point that more difficult than just acknowledging pain is opening ourselves to it and working with it—a sentiment shared by approaches such as ACT (Wilson, 2009). The key point is the ability "to bear" painful feelings and it is linked to courage (Gilbert, 2009a). Strength is also linked to the concept of authority—as we will note below when doing compassion exercises.

Warmth and non-judgement

Warmth was discussed in Point 7. Non-judgement really means non-condemning, with the associated problems of "forcing" change, trying to get rid of things, or destroying them. Clearly compassionate people *want* a compassionate and just world. As well articulated in REBT, there is an important distinction between a preference and a must (Dryden, 2009).

Multi-component

People can express different components of compassion; some people can be kind but not very wise; some people can be generous or gentle but not very courageous. The courageous person who rushes to save a child in a fire might not be the

135

kindest or gentlest of people; justice/fairness concerns and caring concerns can conflict (Gilbert, 2005a). People can be kind to others but not themselves; or kind to friends but vicious to enemies. So, it is important to recognize that compassion is complex, requiring considerably more research into its varied textures. In therapy it's important to try to *articulate compassionate strengths a person may already have* and build on those.

Preparing and training one's mind: Mindfulness and soothing breathing rhythm

Over the last 100 years or so there has been growing interest in a variety of spiritual traditions and mind-training practices that originated in non-Western societies. Among these has been interest in a variety of martial arts (judo and karate), movement-focused approaches (e.g., yoga, chi gong, tai chi) and various forms of Buddhism (e.g., Theravada, Mahayana and Zen). Although different schools are associated with different traditions and practices, a common link between them is *training the mind*—and in particular one's attention. These traditions make a distinction between experience and "experiencing experience", awareness and "awareness of awareness". So, for example, I can suffer anxiety but I can also be aware that I'm suffering anxiety. I can think about my anxiety, allow my thoughts and attention to be controlled by my anxiety—or I can observe my anxiety, choose to be with it, accept it but not act on it. I can pay attention to my breathing and focus my attention "through an act of choice".

Stimulated by the Theravadan (Southern Asian) approach to mind training, *mindfulness* (which comes from the ancient Indian Pali word *Sati*—meaning awareness, attention and remembering) and the work of Jon Kabat-Zinn (2005), the last 20 years have seen major efforts to utilize mindfulness training in psychotherapy (Crane, 2009; Didonna, 2009; Hayes et al., 2004; Segal et al., 2002), the therapeutic relationship (Katzow & Safran, 2007; Siegel, 2010; Wilson, 2009) and self-help (Williams, Teasdale, Segal, & Kabat-Zinn, 2007). Mindfulness teaches people how to pay attention to their inner and external worlds, with curiosity, kindness and non-judgement. Non-judgement really means non-critical and non-condemning—it does not mean non-preference. For example, the Dalai Lama would very much like the world to be a more spiritual place; mindful people *want* a more just society. We also often need to *remember* to be mindful.

It is focusing the attention on observing and being "fully present" that is key to mindfulness. So, for example, while driving your car you may ride home but not really remember much of your drive because your mind was thinking about your work or the weekend. To be fully present would mean to be completely aware of the act of driving in the moment. Mindfulness teaches people to be aware that they have an observing mind that can be the focus of attention. So, for example, to engage in actions mindfully means to pay attention, in the present moment with observing, noticing and open attention. Eating an apple mindfully means paying attention to the visual qualities, the textural qualities, taste and the act of swallowing.

The Tibetan Monk, Matthieu Ricard (2003; personal communication, 2008) uses analogies to help us distinguish the contents of our mind from mindful awareness. He notes: a mirror can reflect many things but the mirror is not those things it reflects; a torchlight can shine on many objects and reveal many colours but the light is not the object it lights up; water can contain a poison or a medicine but water is not the poison or medicine. These analogies are designed to help us distinguish the contents of our mind and the process of conscious awareness of the contents. It is becoming more aware of this distinction and "resting in" conscious awareness without judgement or content that is key to mindfulness.

Mindfulness can help us when we try to avoid thinking and feeling about things—called experiential avoidance (Hayes et al., 2004; Wilson, 2009). The avoidance of feeling takes many forms. For example, people who fear intimacy or try to avoid social anxiety associated with closeness may avoid opportunities for relating and doom themselves to aloneness. To avoid feelings of shame, emptiness, anxiety, rage or depression, people may turn to drink or drugs, reckless activities or over-eating. CFT will help people to learn to be "with feelings"; mindfully desensitizing, tolerating and (if appropriate) learning to accept them. Acceptance doesn't mean that anything goes. If you put your hand near the fire it is a good idea to take it away before you damage tissue; if you are in an abusive relationship it is a good idea to get out of it rather than just accept it. So, acceptance needs to be based on wisdom (Wilson, 2009; Linehan, 1993). In psychotherapy, acceptance and tolerance of painful feelings is facilitated by compassionate empathic understanding and validation by the therapist (Wilson, 2009; Leahy, 2005; Linehan, 1993).

Mindfulness can be a process that helps in the development of mentalizing, the ability to stand back, slow down and reflect on one's own mental states and those of others (see Point 4).

Mindfulness also helps us notice and break out of cycles of *rumination*, because we become more aware of our ruminative minds and the harm they can do. This is an important focus because researchers suggest that rumination can fuel the onset and maintenance of a variety of disorders (see pages 63–66).

From an evolutionary perspective mindfulness also nestles against an issue about *self*-awareness; our sense of a separate self-identity and self-evaluation. The social psychologist Mark Leary (2003) wrote a book called the *Curse of the Self*—highlighting that although our sense of being "a self" has various advantages it also has a number of disadvantages. Self-awareness and self-evaluation can underpin pride and shame and a whole range of harmful coping behaviours when trying to protect our sense of self and self-identity. The practice of mindfulness can help us begin to experience the sense of self and its individual identity in different ways—but this is a subject beyond this book.

Mindfulness doesn't just help us deal with some of the problematic aspects of our minds, it can also help us to become more *appreciative* of where we are; we learn to savour the beauty of the clouds, the sunrise or sunset; enjoy simple pleasures such as the taste of food; see wonder in a flower. These pleasures can easily pass us by because we are not present in the moment; our minds are thinking about 101 other things.

Wandering mind

As noted in the "driving your car" example, our minds can be everywhere except where we are; they can focus on worries, plan future projects and activities, anticipate arguments and plan counter arguments, look forward to holidays, day dream or ruminate and so on. These mental processes have a range of effects on our bodies and mental states. Mindfulness helps us to become aware of this.

Mindfulness is particularly useful to explain to people in order to help them deal with things that interfere with various practices, particularly those relating to behavioural experiments and imagery. These practices are typically difficult for people because our minds wander all over the place especially if we're agitated, preoccupied or anxious. It is therefore important and helpful to teach people that it is natural and normal for their minds to wander. Indeed, recent research suggests that this wandering mind, flitting from idea to idea, scene to scene, and theme to theme, might actually be the source of human creativity and originality. So, you can positively frame the wandering mind in terms of having a creative mind—rather than seeing it as a problem.

Mindfulness teaches us to become aware of the mind when it wanders and gently, kindly and without judgement or criticism bring it back on task. This "noticing and return, noticing and return, noticing and return . . ." *is* one of the key elements of mindfulness. We are learning to pay attention to the way our minds generate thoughts and feelings. The therapist constantly reassures the person that a wandering mind *is not a problem*, because the focus of mindfulness is simply to become aware, to pay attention and to remember to notice, and focus one's attention. People can get discouraged by noticing *how much* their mind wanders and how difficult it is to focus on the task. However, the therapist explains that the fact they are noticing just how much their mind is wandering is not an indication that they can't do it but that they *actually are doing it!* That's all mindfulness is—noticing and returning the attention—it is not trying to empty the mind of thoughts, which is the common misunderstanding.

Not only is mindfulness useful in its own right (in some therapies it is the key focus of the therapy; Crane, 2009; Segal et al., 2002), but it is a major element of many compassion-focused exercises. For example, compassionate thinking, behaviour and imagery can be generated and enacted mindfully.

Soothing breathing rhythm

The Dalai Lama often points out that in order for us to use our minds effectively we need to cultivate "calm mind". In the martial arts the focus is on learning how to be in the moment, and fight or defend from a point of stillness rather than rage, terror or desire to humiliate and harm. These are, of course, ideals to aim for but they recognize the importance of teaching people practices to work with bodily arousal. One of these in CFT is called "soothing breathing rhythm". You can find the full instructions for the exercise in *The Compassionate Mind* book (Gilbert, 2009a, pages 224–228). You may wish to make your own tapes/CDs that you give to people and you can find this and other compassion focused exercises on my CD (Gilbert, 2007d).

Once sitting comfortably, with straight posture and feet flat on the ground, people are encouraged to breath a little deeper than normal and notice or look for a rhythm of their breathing, which helps them feel they are *slowing down*. In some breathing tasks participants are asked to count, whereas in soothing breathing rhythm we suggest paying attention to this process of slowing and being sensitive to the link between bodily feelings and breathing. If you want to contrast it for clients then ask them to breath quickly and notice the bodily changes, and then change back to soothing breathing rhythm again.

We can combine soothing breathing rhythm with various relaxation exercises and body scans. However, in CFT we regard tension as part of the protection system; tension developed to protect us and prepare us for action. So, the instruction is that tension is something to let go of "for which it is grateful". In other words don't see "tension" as something bad to be got rid of because this creates an unhelpful mind state. Rather, it is about being grateful to tension, but it's not necessary now and we can let it go.

Some people actually find soothing breathing rhythm quite alarming and therefore that suggests slow desensitization. When working with a group of people who had chronic mental-health problems, a number of them did not want to do any breathing work at first. After a group discussion it was decided that we could do mindful focusing using tennis balls (Gilbert & Procter, 2006), which led to amusing comments by clients, "Hold on to your balls, we are going mindful!" By the end of the therapy, though, they had got the hang of soothing breathing rhythm.

Attention to physiological and bodily processes is important (Ogden et al., 2006). Placing this work in the context of the "three circles model" can help people become quite innovative once they know what they're trying to do "for their brains".

Practise when it is easy

Behaviour therapists are very familiar with the concept of graded tasks and gradual exposure. It is the same with all of the exercises in this book. Moreover, you need to explain to people that they should practise *when it is easy*—when they are feeling good! For example, if you want to learn to swim it's a good idea to practise in the shallow end of the swimming pool in pleasantly warm water. It's not a good idea to learn if you fall overboard in a storm. You should learn to drive by practising on the back streets or in a disused car park—not on the motorway; don't try to run a marathon when you first start trying to get physically fit. All these analogies help people recognize that some of their techniques won't work for them when they are at their worst even though that's when they want them for—but the reasons for this are logical—they haven't developed the skills (or maybe brain systems). The more people practise when they feel *well* and then gradually introduce it to times of difficulty the more likely practice will work. So, as therapists you will be helping people to think about the *easiest* times to practise to begin with, get a practice routine for the exercises below, and then gradually take that practice into more difficult situations.

As with mindfulness, of course, much depends on remembering "in the moment" to bring one's skills to bear. So, for example, when people have been practising compassionate thinking, it's important for them to remember and try to shift to that mode of thinking when distressed or in a conflict. It's a time to remember to take a few breaths and focus on the compassionate self or compassionate images (see below).

Introducing imagery

As noted above CFT rests on a very clear evolutionary and neuroscience model that is shared with the client. It seeks to de-pathologize and de-shame by being explicit that we have problems because of basic brain design, historical, current contextual and social difficulties. Helping people gain a deeper understanding of why their problems are "not their fault" in a blaming and shaming sense, while at the same time recognizing the importance of "taking responsibility", is key to CFT. We have also spent time looking at the compassion circles and in particular the importance of compassionate attention, compassionate thinking, compassionate behaviour and *being motivated* to approach difficulties and our sense of self, compassionately. Imagery is contextualized within this overall framework. I do become worried when I hear therapists just trying "a bit of compassionate imagery" and finding that it does not work so well (see Point 29).

CFT explains imagery within the three circles model (Point 6) and the brain diagram (Figure 11) so that people really understand why they are engaging in imagery as a training exercise. Imagery has been used in a variety of psychotherapies and it is recognized that it can be more powerful than verbal work (Hall, Hall, Stradling, & Young, 2006; Singer, 2006; Stopa, 2009). It can help create positive perceptions of others (Crisp & Turner, 2009) and is used in classical conditioning paradigms (Dadds, Bovbjerg, Redd, & Cutmore, 1997). Imagery re-scripting is a very powerful means of working with PTSD and coping with intrusive memories (Brewin et al., 2009). It is important in many forms of Buddhist meditations to create certain states of mind (Vessantara, 1993) and for CFT (Gilbert, 2009c).

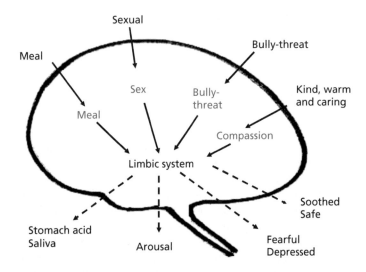

Figure 11 The brain diagram. Reproduced with kind permission from
Gilbert, P. (2009a) *The Compassionate Mind*. London:
Constable & Robinson and Oaklands, CA: New Harbinger

It is important to help people understand the power of
imagery by using simple examples. Below is how we explore it
in CFT. First we draw out a rough shape of the brain (see
Figure 11) with the client and then go through this type of
explanation, writing in the words as one speaks:

Guidance

Imagine that you are very hungry and you see a lovely meal.
What happens in your body? (*invite a response*) The sight of
the meal stimulates an area of your brain that sends
messages to your body so that your mouth starts to water
and your stomach acids get going. Spend a moment really
thinking about that. Now, suppose that you're very hungry
but there isn't any food in the house, so you close your eyes
and *just imagine* a wonderful meal. What happens in your

body then? Again, spend a moment really thinking about that. Well, those images *that you deliberately create in your mind* can also send messages to parts of your brain that send messages to your body, so again your mouth will water and your stomach acids will get going. Remember, this time, that there is no meal: it's only an image that you've created in your mind, yet that image is capable of stimulating those physiological systems in your body that makes your saliva flow. Take a moment to think about that.

Now let's look at another example, something that many of us may have come across: you see something sexy on TV. Now this may stimulate an area of your brain that affects your body, leading to arousal. Equally, of course, we know that even if we're alone in the house we can just imagine something sexy and that can affect our body. The reason for this is that the *image alone* can stimulate physiological systems in our brain in an area called the *pituitary*, which will release hormones into our body.

The point of this story is that thoughts and images are very powerful ways of stimulating reactions in our brains and our body. Take a moment and really think about that, because this insight will link to other ideas to come. Images that we deliberately create in our mind and with our thinking will stimulate our physiology and body systems.

Now let's think of a more threat-linked example. Suppose someone is bullying you. They are always pointing out your mistakes or dwelling on things you are unhappy with, or telling you that you are no good and there is no point in you trying anything, or being angry with you. This will affect your stress systems, and your level of cortisol, the stress hormone, will increase. How do you feel if people criticize you? How does it feel in your body? Spend a moment thinking about this. Their unpleasantness will make you feel anxious, upset and unhappy because the threat emotion systems in your brain have been triggered. However, as we have suggested, and here is the point—*our own thoughts and images can do the same*. If you are constantly putting yourself down this can also activate your stress systems and trigger the emotional systems in your brain that can lead to feeling anxious, angry and down. Our own thoughts can affect parts of our brain that give rise to *stressful and unpleasant feelings*. They can certainly tone down positive feelings. Whoever had a feeling of joy, happiness, contentment or well-being from being criticized! If we develop a self-critical style then we are constantly stimulating our threat system and will understandably feel constantly under threat. Self-criticism, then, stimulates the threat system. This is no different from saying that sexual thoughts and feelings will stimulate your sexual system, and the thoughts of a lovely meal will stimulate your eating system.

In contrast, if we are upset that we've made a mistake or experienced a setback in life, and somebody is very kind, validating and understanding of us, this will help to settle feelings of stress; we feel supported and cared about. Therefore using the same ideas in regard to a meal, a sexual fantasy, or a self-criticism, learning to be self-compassionate and generating compassionate thoughts and images can help us self-soothe when we feel threatened.

Using these instructions clearly, helps to contextualize the use of imagery. You can ask, "Can you see why compassionate imagery and thoughts might be a useful practice for you?" The more you focus on the practices and physiological aspects, the more you can work around certain resistances (see Point 29; Gilbert & Irons, 2005).

Explaining and exploring imagery

Some people feel they are poor imagers. So, you can invite them to do an experiment. First, sit quietly and then say "bicycle", and ask them to describe what popped into their mind; "ice cream" or "party", then ask them what popped into their mind. Imagery can be automatic. If they say they didn't get anything ask, "What does a bicycle look like? How many wheels? Where are the brakes? and so on—and when they answer then ask, "How did you come to that?" Or you can ask someone to tell you what they had for breakfast—and again ask them how they could respond to you. Sometimes people have images but they just don't realize what they are or people think that they need to be clear Polaroid-like pictures rather than a vague sense of something. However, some people are, of course, more "visual" than others.

Different images will have different emotional textures because of various associations. Emotions in images associated with trauma will be quite different from images associated with happy times. Some trauma images can have clear sensory memory of certain details (Ogden et al., 2006). So, the sensory (visual or auditory) elements of an image can be distinguished from its emotional elements. In compassionate imagery we are creating images that will gradually link to emotional elements.

Compassionate imagery

Imagery can be a basis for compassion reflection, providing ideas for compassionate thinking and behaviour and also meditation. There is no imagery in pure mindfulness; it is just about paying attention to this moment, the flow of our internal and external worlds, without judgement or wishing for other than it is. Compassion focusing, however, has various laid-out practices utilizing specific forms of imagery. When we introduce imagery work we do so with the information:

Guidance

We're going to try some imagery but before we do a few words of caution. Some people take to imagery and others struggle. First, if you're one of those who struggle a bit then remember that it's *your intention* to develop more compassion that's important and not the feeling or the clarity of the image particularly. Second, people often think they have to create clear images whereas the images may be very fleeting, or hazy. We don't create Polaroid images in our minds. Sometimes we need to practise imagery. We can do this, for example, by looking at, say, a bowl of fruit or flowers in a vase, and closing our eyes and then imagining what we've just seen. Try to be playful and curious; try out different things and see what works for you.

Remind people about other likely problems that they may meet such as a wandering mind. Reassure them that the key is simply to notice and return one's attention to the tasks. You will be checking constantly to see if people engage their self-monitoring system and try to judge whether they are "doing it right" or getting a certain type of feeling, or if it is helping. Imaging voice tones and content can be easier for some people.

19

Creating a safe place

A useful first imagery exercise is "creating a safe place" where the person feels comfortable, safe, soothed and calmed; a place they might want to be. To begin with, it is useful to start by sitting comfortably and going through a soothing breathing rhythm and a short relaxation exercise. If your clients don't like the breathing exercise then just ask them to sit quietly for a few moments. All imagery of this sort should be done seriously but "playfully", noting "wandering mind" and that images are often fleeting and impressionistic. Keep in mind that types of imagery can be very difficult if people are very anxious or agitated and physical activity is usually better at those times. Here are some guides:

Guiding imagery

In this imagery we are going to try to *create a place* in our mind—a place that could give you the *feeling of safeness, calmness*. If you are depressed those might be difficult feelings to generate, but the act of trying, and the sense of it being the sort of place you would like to be, is the important thing. So, remember, it is the act of trying the practice that is important, feelings may follow later.

The place may be a beautiful wood where the leaves of the trees dance gently in the breeze. Powerful shafts of light caress the ground with brightness. Imagine a wind blowing gently on your face and a sense of the light dancing in front of you. Hear the rustle of the leaves on the trees; imagine a smell of woodiness or a sweetness of the air. Your place may be a beautiful beach with a crystal blue sea stretching out to the horizon where it meets the ice blue sky. Under foot is soft, white, fine sand that is silky to the touch. You can hear the gentle hushing of the waves on the sand. Imagine the sun on your face, sense the light dancing in diamond specks on the water, imagine the soft sand under your feet as your toes dig into it and feel a light breeze gently touch your face. Your safe place may be by a log fire where you can hear the crackle of the logs burning and smell the wood smoke. These are examples of possible pleasant places that may bring a sense of pleasure to you, but the key focus is on a feeling of safeness for you. These examples are only suggestions and yours might be different to these.

It helps your attention if you practise focusing on each of your senses; what you can imagine seeing, feeling, hearing and any other sensory aspect.

When you bring your safe place to mind, allow your body to relax. Think about your facial expression; allow it to have a soft smile of pleasure at being there.

It is also useful to imagine that as this is your own unique safe place, created by you, so *the place itself takes joy in your being there*. Explore how it might feel if your safe place takes pleasure in your being there. Explore your feelings when you imagine this place is happy with you being there.

We use the "*the place itself takes joy in your being there*" because, as noted above, caring evolved with motives of being valued and cared for and it is those systems (feeling wanted) that one is trying to stimulate. Go through each sensory focus slowly with plenty of space. Keep in mind that we are using imagery *not to* escape or avoid but to help people practise bringing soothing to their minds. Keep in mind, too, that these

exercises are to try out—experiment and see what happens—
and also for training.

Compassionate colour

In using compassionate imagery you may find that sometimes
people like to start off with imagining a compassionate colour.
Usually these colours are pastel rather than dark. In groups it is
interesting to note people's different colours—which may
change over the therapy. Use frequent pauses and go slowly.

Guidance

Engage in your soothing breathing rhythm and when ready
imagine a colour that you associate with compassion, or a
colour that conveys some sense of warmth and kindness.
Again, it might only be a fleeting sense of colour(s) but
when you are ready, imagine your compassionate colour(s)
surrounding you. Then, imagine this entering through your
heart area and slowly through your body. As this happens
try to focus on this colour as having wisdom, strength and
warmth/kindness with a key quality of total kindness. Create
a facial expression of kindness on your own face as you do
this exercise. Feel that the colour wants to help you—
imagine that its sole intention is to heal you and that it
wishes for your happiness; focus on sensing that intention.

Note the key here is practising the feeling of being cared for (in
this case it is by a colour—which can be less threatening than
imagining a compassionate person, see Point 29).

One person noted that when she used compassion to help her
face up to difficult decisions her chosen colour became stronger.
This person was good at experimenting and seeing what worked
for her; listening to her own intuitive wisdom. So, she began
to think about her compassion colours as helping her with
different things.

Varieties of compassion focused imagery

In Mahayana Buddhism there is a huge literature on various types of compassion imagery (Leighton, 2003; Vessantara, 1993). However, in the West, the most common form of compassion imagery has been taken from the Theravadan traditions and in particular those associated with loving(friendly)-kindness (Salzberg, 1995). For example, Kabat-Zinn (2005, pp. 285–296) gives a brief introduction and overview of loving-kindness meditations that involves: "Remembering others being kind to you; recalling times when you were kind to others; and if you struggle to recall others being kind to you then imagine figures being kind to you". Loving-kindness visualizing is now used in various self-help ways (see Germer, 2009; Salzberg, 1995). It is important to note, too, that traditions within other spiritual traditions and psychotherapy have focused on inter-personal imagery associated with being helped, kindness, meeting a wise, supportive other or friend, and receiving compassion (Frederick & McNeal, 1999).

Compassion focused exercises and imagery stimulate particular brain systems, especially the affiliative and soothing—oxytocin/endorphin—system (see pages 48–50; also Longe et al., 2010; Rockliff et al., 2008). At root CMT is concerned with physiological regulation using exercises to help to bring on line particular types and patterns of positive affect that enhance feelings of safeness, reassurance and well-being and tone down the threat system. (Oxytocin and endorphins can tone down activity in the—threat-processing—amygdala.) Compassion focused exercises can be orientated in four main ways:

1 *Developing the inner compassionate self*: In these exercises we focus on creating a sense of becoming a compassionate self, just like actors do if they are trying to get into a role.

2 *Compassion flowing out from you to others*: In these exercises we focus on filling our minds with compassionate feelings for other people.

3 *Compassion flowing into you*: In these exercises we focus our minds on opening up to the kindness of others. This is to open the mind and stimulate areas of our brain that are responsive to the kindness of others.

4 *Compassion to yourself*: This is linked to developing feelings, thoughts and experiences that are focused on compassion to oneself. Life is often very difficult and learning how to generate self-compassion can be very helpful during these times, particularly to help us with our emotions.

Recall that compassion involves a number of *attributes* and key *skills*, e.g., attending in compassionate ways, generating and practising compassionate thinking, acting in compassionate ways, and generating compassionate feeling (see Point 16; and Gilbert, 2009a, pp. 191–210). All of these will be enhanced with practice, just as if we were learning to play golf or the piano.

The basic idea is that it is so easy to get trapped and caught in cycles of thinking, imaging and feeling things when threatened, anxious or angry. Therefore, it is helpful to learn to practise generating states of mind (activating systems in our brain) that can tone down the threat system. Clients can learn how to:

- accept feelings for what they are (e.g., archetypal)—rather than try to avoid them or for them to become intolerable, overwhelming or frightening;
- learn to be compassionate and understanding to them, depersonalize and de-shame (I am not the only one), and switch to a compassion focus if threatened;

- recognize unhelpful self-criticism and refocus on self-compassion;
- recognize unhelpful rumination and replace it with helpful compassion focusing and practice.

Compassion focused work is a way of shifting, redirecting, taking control over and deliberately enabling oneself to move into emotion and feeling systems that are conducive to well-being. It is not easy, of course, and requires practice.

Developing the compassionate self

The different parts of us

It is important to discuss with people that we are basically pattern generators (Gilbert, 2009a) and that we can create many different patterns of brain activity in ourselves and then see these as different parts of ourselves (see Point 4). There is the pattern that emerges with anger that we can call the angry "part" or "self". The angry part of us thinks, feels and wants to act in a certain way. Or we might focus on the anxious pattern, or a "being in love" or a "falling out of love" pattern. We have thousands of different potential patterns within ourselves. Developing the compassionate self and the compassionate pattern can be key to helping deal with "this multiplicity of mind" and, of course, the unpleasant, difficult or harmful patterns (parts of self) that arise in us. Compassion can have a soothing quality on anger and anxiety, but it will also help us develop courage to face these and learn how to tolerate them or act on them appropriately.

Now, there are many different compassionate-self-developing exercises and for any one person it's not always clear as to which are the best exercises to start with. So, to some extent, we have to experiment. However, a helpful place to start (especially for abused people who struggle to imagine others being compassionate to them) is to focus on developing the sense of being and becoming a compassionate person oneself.

There are many ways in which this can be done and there are many traditions that use these kinds of techniques. For example, certain schools of Buddhism suggest that the seeds of many types of self exist within "oneself" and it is how we nurture and focus on them that is important. If we want to be a musician, we practice playing an instrument, or to be a good driver, we practice driving. However, for the most part we mindlessly allow the environment to "grow and shape our minds", so that we are simply responding and fitting into the social environments in which we live. However, we can choose *to cultivate* other aspects of ourselves. The key, then, is to think about what we want to practise, what/who we want to become within ourselves. Typically, we don't think that we can deliberately practise becoming a certain type of person—but we can, we just have to decide to do it and then put in the time to practise.

Imagining the compassionate self

There is a long history of using imagery to prepare for stressful events and for coping. For example, we might practise imagining oneself coping with a future stressful event and then imagine feeling pleased. Compassionate imagery is really just an extension of that behavioural work, based on a clear understanding of there being different types of positive emotion-regulation system. Another way to approach this is using *acting* techniques (Gilbert, 2009a). Key here, however, is imagery of a particular type of self and self-identity. There is increasing evidence that the kind of self we try to become will influence our well-being and social relationships, and compassionate rather than self-focused self-identities are associated with the better outcomes (Crocker & Canevello, 2008). So, here it is about becoming a certain type of person. You can explain the following to people:

Guidance

If you were an actor learning to act, you might pay attention to key elements of a character. This might be a character who is angry, depressed, anxious, happy, joyful "James or Jane Bond", and of course compassionate. So, as a keen actor, what you would try to do would be to try to create certain feelings, thoughts and motives within yourself, try *to be* or become that character—live it from the inside. To do this you might pay attention to the way this character thinks and sees the world, the tone of voice of the character, the postures and the general bearing of the character, the kinds of things they say and the way they say them. Okay, so the character we are going to become is a compassionate one, this is the part of us we want to feed, nurture and develop.

Now consider all the key qualities you think make up a compassionate person. Visit and rest in them in your mind. Here are four key qualities:

1   Wisdom derived from personal experiences, maturity and gaining insight into the nature of things and life's difficulties. Your compassionate self knows that we "all just find ourselves in this life" with a brain that we did not design and early life experience that shape us that we did not choose. We are all trying to find happiness and avoid suffering. We have minds that are at times chaotic and full of conflicting thoughts and feelings. Thus, wisdom comes from understanding these aspects.
2   Strength, as in fortitude and courage. Focus on feelings of maturity and a sense of inner authority. Imagine yourself with calm confidence and a sense of authority.
3   Great warmth and kindness.
4   Non-condemning nor critically (self)-judgemental but with a sense of responsibility (and desire) to help or for change.

A very useful thing to do is also to *imagine yourself expanding* as if your wisdom is making you bigger, more dominant or powerful, in a *mature compassionate* way. You may even think of yourself as older. Now, you may want to practise focusing on each of these and imagine having these qualities, noting what they feel like and any effect this has on your body. So the practice is:

- Find somewhere you can sit quietly and will not be disturbed and focus on your soothing breathing rhythm. When you feel that your body has slowed down (even slightly), and you are ready for your practice, imagine that *you are* a very deeply compassionate person.
- Think of all the qualities that you would ideally have as that compassionate person. Let's go through them.
- Focus on your desires to become "a compassionate person" and think, act and feel compassionately. Next, imagine yourself with each of the qualities noted: imagine being calm and having wisdom (spend time just on this). Imagine yourself being sensitive with an ability to tolerate difficulties (spend time on just that). Imagine being warm and kind (spend time on just that). Imagine being non-condemning but also wanting to help, relieve suffering and produce change and "flourishing".
- Try to create a facial expression of compassion, maybe a slight smile or maybe a different expression to suit you.
- Imagine yourself expanding as if you are becoming more powerful, mature, wise and confident authority.
- Pay attention to your body as you bring this part of you to the fore.
- Spend a moment just feeling this expansion and warmth in your body.
- Spend one minute, more if you are able, thinking about your tone of voice and the kind of things you'd say or the kind of things you'd do or want to do.
- Spend one minute, more if you are able, thinking about your pleasure in being able to be kind.

Remember, it *doesn't matter if you feel you have these qualities or not*, just imagine that you have them. See in your mind yourself having them, and work through them steadily, playfully and slowly. Sometimes we notice how each quality can affect our bodies differently. Remember that you may just get glimmers of things because your mind wanders or you can't really focus. This is very typical of what happens, just as if we were trying to learn to play the piano—we'd be all fingers and thumbs to start with. Regular practice will help.

You at your best

Another way you can access and practice your compassionates self is to spend a moment and remind yourself of a time when you felt compassionate; that is, calm and wise and wanting to help. You can think of your compassionate self as "you at your best" imagining that inner sense of calm and supportive voice. Use a compassionate expression when you recall this. Don't focus on a time when someone was very distressed because that might focus you on the distress. The aim is to focus on your feelings of *wanting to help* and your kindness.

Compassion under the duvet

Ideally, try to practise "becoming the compassionate self" each day. If our lives are busy we can start by learning what can be called "compassion under the duvet". Thus, when you wake up in the morning, try to spend a few minutes practising becoming your compassionate self. As you lie in bed, bring a compassionate expression to your face, focus on your *real desire* to be wise and compassionate; remember inside you, you have the capacity for wisdom and strength, but you have to create space for it. Even two minutes a day, if practised every day, may have an effect. You can also practise when you stand at the bus stop or are just lying in the bath. After all, how often do we lie in the warmth of a bath and not really notice because our mind is wandering over all kinds of things—mostly worries or things we need to do! This is not very relaxing! You may then find you'll want to practice for longer periods of time or even perhaps find places where you can train more. Whenever you are aware of it, even sitting in a meeting you can use soothing breathing and focus on becoming the wisest, compassionate, calm mature self.

The importance of personal practice and (an example of) compassionate thinking

It is increasingly recognized that therapists would benefit from some kind of personal practice of the therapy they practise (Bennett-Levy & Thwaites, 2007). CFT strongly endorses this and advises CF therapists to practise mindful and compassionate self-focusing and meditations as often as possible. We also advise utilizing this in regard to one's own difficulties. So, here is an example that illuminates compassionate thinking, but used on yourself. Suppose you are having difficulties with clients and feeling anxious or self-critical, try the following. Assume that you can generate some alternative thoughts of:

- *It is understandable to struggle with some clients because we are dealing with complex suffering and tragedies* (validation).
- *Many therapists have difficulties with some clients* (common humanity).
- *I can remember clients who have done well with me* (bringing to mind the specific memories; refocusing attention).
- *Learning to tolerate these anxieties and concerns is important for me* (thinking of what is the developmental task).
- *Turning to others for supervision, advice and help when I'm struggling is important for me* (opening oneself to be helped, avoiding feeling ashamed of difficulties, and engaging in the compassionate behaviour of help seeking).

Read these thoughts through and rate them (say, 1–10) for how helpful they are to you. Now spend one minute in soothing breathing rhythm and one minute on becoming your compassionate self; feel yourself grow into it. Really focus on a sense of inner calmness, wisdom, motivation to help, kindness, the warmth and tone of your voice. When you feel you are in contact with "that self", read the thoughts in italics again but this time *slowly* and focus on as much kindness and warmth as you can and less on the content or logic of the alternatives. Now rate how helpful they seem to you. See if you can spot the difference between the two ways of working on your anxieties. In our second read through, I have tried to help you activate an affect system and then engage with your alternatives. If it has worked (and you followed through on the suggestions) you may have noticed a slightly different feeling arising from reading the alternatives compassionately.

So, this helps us to recognize the importance of personal practice; with each day we try to become more of a compassionate self. Try the practice before seeing clients. Try it too, the next time you have a conflict with someone—take a minute (or more) for soothing breathing rhythm and then on becoming the compassionate self and then really focus on what a compassionate position, way of thinking and behaving, would be. Notice how this might break up more negative ruminations. Indeed, all the exercises here can be used for personal practice.

22

Compassionate chair work

Many therapies use chairs where different "parts of the person" can enact their thoughts and feelings. So, for example, you could have an angry chair where the client simply engages with their anger and lets their anger speak, or an anxious chair, where a person engages with their anxiety and voices their anxious thoughts and feelings. You could have a self-critical chair, where the person becomes the self-critic. In some approaches you can enable clients to switch chairs and dialogue with these various parts of the self, an approach well developed by Leslie Greenberg (Elliott et al., 2003; Greenberg, Rice, & Elliott, 1993; Whelton & Greenberg, 2005).

CFT uses chair work a lot but the key focus is on the compassion chair and *building up* the feelings, tolerance, insights and strengths of this part of the self (Gilbert, 2000a). So, if we work with a self-critical part, we invite the person to respond with compassion by sitting in a facing chair and becoming the compassionate self (as outlined above). In straight CBT you might invite the person to become more balanced in their thoughts and reflect and talk to the angry or self-critical part of self—moving back and forth between the chairs. In CFT, though, it is cultivating the *motivation* and *feeling* to try to compassionately help the angry, anxious or self-critical self that is key.

So, discuss with the client the nature of the different parts of the self (spend time and normalize), and the fact that part of therapy is to strengthen those parts that are capable of growth, change and healing (e.g., the compassionate self). Then you may generate a collaborative agreement on this. If the client agrees, you can then choose which chairs and which roles the

167

client can be active in; then start with "becoming the part" you want to work on. Ask the person to recall a time when they felt that part (e.g., anger, anxiety, self-criticism or sadness) and give voice to that part—noting feeling and bodily experiences of that part. Start with mild examples and work up according to the abilities of the client.

Next, the client switches to a facing chair. Maybe they walk around a bit first to give plenty of space to disengage from the part they are working with and to be able to create a sense of a compassionate self. Do this before engaging in any dialogues or expressing any feelings. Use soothing breathing rhythm in the compassion chair, with mindfulness. You might want to give the following guidance—spoken slowly and with pauses (. . . .).

Guidance

In your compassion chair now, engage your soothing breathing rhythm and feel your body slowing down. Now focus on becoming "you at your best" . . . . Maybe remember a time when you felt calmer, wiser and kind . . . . Imagine all the qualities you would ideally like to have as a compassionate person . . . . Notice how thinking about them can help you feel in touch with them . . . . Allow yourself to have a compassionate expression . . . . Calmly and gently visualize yourself having wisdom, maturity, authority and strength as you sit there . . . . With your soothing rhythm, as your body is slowing down, feel yourself becoming the compassionate self.

When some sense of contact with a compassionate self is made you then invite them to spend time *just feeling compassion for* the angry, anxious, sad or self-critical part (*check that the self-critical part is not the voice of an abuser, as this is a different process here, see below*). If the person feels pulled by the other chair so that they start to feel angry or self-critical, or overpowered, then just break contact with the chair and refocus on "becoming the compassionate self"—similar to a gradual exposure approach. The focus is *on building the compassionate self* so that it can work with the other parts of the self.

Give some time for just reflecting on sending compassion for the angry or self-critical self, etc. What comes up for people when they are compassionate to their anger or to their self-critical self? The compassionate self might then be invited to consider: "What's really upsetting/threatening this (e.g., angry or self-critical) 'self' (thus locating the issue as threat processing). What would the compassionate self like to say or do? Imagine that the angry self or self-critical self is healed, no longer threatened—How would it then feel?—How would that help?" Just hold here. The client's mind will wander so just bring them back by repeating the guidance above. "Imagine what happens if this part gets all the compassion they need. Imagine that the threats settles for it."

Keep your major focus on the compassion: parent-like, wise and mature, with authority and inner strength. CMT is mostly focused on strengthening this brain state, making it easier to trigger and giving it a retrieval advantage (Brewin, 2006). Help the client identify with "wanting to become more like this"— build compassion into his/her self-identity. Use the motto "we become what we feed/practice". Focus on "training our minds". As noted above (pages 112–113) there is increasing evidence that the kind of self we try to become will influence our well-being and social relationships (Crocker & Canevello, 2008).

In compassion focused work it's always about building this part of the self as a counter to the threat system with its anger, anxiety and self-criticism, etc. You will find that some clients start to be able to tolerate their negative emotions better and can remind themselves of their compassionate voice/feelings and thoughts.

The compassionate self does not try to "get rid" or "sooth away" these other parts of the self but takes them seriously as important "voices" and works compassionately with them. One key exception to this is if the inner critic is felt to be "the voice of a past abuser"—then this is marked as the "not self" and invited to leave or handled assertively, or with empty chair work, or with trauma re-scripting—or however the person feels is best for them. Space does not allow extensive discussion of this but there are literatures on working with these internalized "voices" (Ogden et al., 2006).

Focusing of the compassionate self

A very important way of compassionately engaging with different and problematic parts of the self (problematic brain patterns) is in imagery. When people have practised this a little, they can learn to *focus* their compassionate self.

Guidance

Suppose you're very anxious about something. Sit quietly and engage in your breathing and then imagine yourself as a compassionate person. When you can feel that expanding and growing inside of you, then imagine you can see your anxious self in front of you. Look at his or her facial expression; note the feelings rushing through them. Just sit and feel compassion, and send compassionate feelings out to that anxious self. Try to surround that anxious self in compassion and understanding of the torment of anxiety. For now you are not trying to do anything other than experience compassion and acceptance for your anxiety. Imagine giving as much compassion and understanding as that anxious part needs. You may want to imagine what happens to the anxious part when it actually has all of the understanding and support it needs.

Interestingly, a colleague, Fay Adams from the Holy Island Buddhist Centre in Scotland, sent me a book, where I discovered this exercise is not dissimilar to an approach developed by an eleventh-century female Buddhist teacher Machig Labdron (1055–1145)! She advocated an imagery exercise where one turned one's body into nectar to feed one's demons (one's problems or problematic parts of the self) (Allione, 2008).

As in chair work, if people feel they're becoming anxious or being pulled into the anxiety, then just break contact with the image and ask them to refocus on their breathing and the sense of being "an expanding, wise and strong compassionate self; them at their best". When they make contact with that part of themselves again then they can re-engage with the anxious self (or whatever part of self they are working on). So, gently and kindly, they begin to be able to tolerate, accept and feel compassion for their (say) anxious self. As this happens they can notice what happens to the image of their anxious self. It might change or even move away—go with whatever feels right for them.

You can also begin to invite the person to follow the imagery onwards. So, for example, they may see themselves becoming anxious, looking at their anxiety with compassion—but then watch themselves coming out of the anxiety and learning to be proud of having got through it. They can note what helped and what might help next time. The therapist might invite the compassionate self to think about what they would like to say to the anxious self—not only while anxious but also in the scene where they are no longer anxious. Moving people through imagery of engaging the problem, experiencing the problem, coping with the problem and recovering—all through the eyes mentality of the compassionate self—can be helpful. People may recall doing this in future when they feel anxious again and practise shifting to compassionate self when actually experiencing anxiety.

If you are working on the critical self (e.g., imagining it in front of you) then recall that you do not spend too long focusing and letting (say) the self-criticism "vent" before switching to "compassionate self" because the key is *building the compassionate-self pattern*; getting used to what that feels like. If you're working with self-criticism it is useful to enable the compassionate self to think about what is the threat behind self-criticism, for example, the fear of rejection or letting oneself down. One then directs compassion to that underlying threat and fear.

You can explain to clients how, sometimes, we feel that the critical-self "voice" is an echo of someone who was hurtful to us in some way; maybe the mother's or father's voice in our head. The compassionate action here is realizing that this type of self-criticism has come from someone else who may have lacked compassion, and their hurtful words and/or actions were not in the client's best interests. If the client were caring for a child would they treat them like that? If not then how would they *like* to treat a child? So, the client can compassionately recognize that as a child they would have listened to the other person and may have believed and internalized those hurtful things. However, now with the compassionate self, they recognize that was unfair and hurtful and they do not want to continue this same, unkind process. Sometimes the compassionate self wants to be very assertive to a person from the past who was unkind or abusive. In this context use an empty chair or bring to mind the actual person in question and verbalise the assertive feelings (Hackmann, 2005).

Re-scripting

Once a person has some experience of creating the compassionate self, which acts as a grounding (a focus) for a particular affect-processing system and social mentality activation, you can use this to engage in re-scripting (e.g., Brewin et al., 2009; Wheatley et al., 2007). For example, supposing somebody wants to work with a difficult memory, you can first create the compassionate self and then begin to approach the memory as a "scene in one's mind's eye". The person holds the compassionate position as they watch (check on their breathing and facial expressions). They then imagine the scene unfolding. Then, gradually, with the compassionate self they might bring new things into the scene (e.g., helpers) and begin to decide on new endings. The compassionate self can offer any support to the self that they see in their memory. They can also make up the most fantastical endings (Brewin et al., 2009). Keep in mind that the compassionate self really controls the working through this memory and therefore recognizes its power to do so. At the same time the therapist may be speaking very gently and calmly to the client, acting as a soothing mentor—moving into the memory and then back to the compassionate self according to what is feeling safe for the client. In this way, through the compassionate self, you are bringing a new type of mentalizing.

Compassionate focusing and mentalizing

In Point 4 we discussed in detail the importance of mentalizing abilities and competencies. It is possible (although we must await good research evidence) that developing the compassionate self and focusing it on difficulties (either in chair work or imagination) facilitates mentalizing abilities. There may be many reasons for this, including the following:

- You are slowing the client down and focusing on the body sensations with soothing breathing rhythm.
- You are deliberately holding their attention in the compassionate self and therefore at a distance from the anxious, critical or angry self, or difficult memories—which makes reflecting "safer".
- You are specifically activating the care-giving mentality, which brings on line competencies for empathy and motives to help and be supportive.
- You are creating an emotional tone (caring), which counteracts threat-based emotions of anxiety, anger, etc.
- The compassionate self is specifically de-shaming.
- A compassionate-self focus offers a new focus for attention if you are helping the person with attentional control.
- You are helping to desensitize their ability to engage with different aspects of the self by giving them control—such that they can pull back into focusing on the compassionate self and the soothing breathing rhythm if they feel over-whelmed.

- From within the compassionate self you can generate alternative thoughts and insights, which are based on "wisdom and genuine care" and that can be used subsequently.
- You may sit next to them (if they wish) offering guidance in a very slow, calming way acting like a soothing (attachment) object.
- By discussing the issues of becoming the compassionate self you are gradually engaging a person in the desire for that "stronger, wiser, calmer compassionate self" identity to emerge.

There may well be other reasons too—for example, we know that there are differences in brain patterns when we approach potential shaming material with either a self-critical or a self-reassuring orientation (Longe et al., 2010). As suggested for nearly 2500 years by Buddhist thinkers and practitioners, compassion transforms and integrates the mind.

24

Compassion flowing out

There is now increasing evidence that developing compassion for others is highly conducive to well-being (e.g., Frederickson et al., 2008; Lutz et al., 2008). Sometimes people will find this exercise much easier than developing compassion for themselves, but there are some key things to think about here. Sometimes people will develop what looks like compassion but actually it's submissive appeasing, cultivating "niceness" or wanting to be nice to be liked. While various elements of this exist in all of us, some individuals lack mentalizing abilities, genuine empathy about what other people really need (as opposed to want), and can find difficulties in being assertive or putting down boundaries—a problem sometimes in parenting. A completely different problem arises with people who have unprocessed anger. These individuals find compassion difficult, partly because they feel that being a compassionate person means *getting rid* of anger, it is not compassionate to *even feel* anger—rather than that compassion is first and foremost about honesty, tolerating and understanding our feelings.

Nonetheless, beginning to focus on compassion flowing out to others can be very helpful. *Memories* can be a good place to begin to try to stimulate these brain systems that we're interested in. Here is an exercise:

Guidance

In this exercise we are going to imagine kindness and compassion flowing from you to others. Sit quietly where you won't be disturbed and focus on your breathing. When that's okay for you, try and recall a time when you felt very kind and caring towards someone (or if you prefer, an animal). Try not to choose a time when that person (or animal) was very distressed because then you are likely to focus on that distress. The idea is to focus on the desires to help and feelings of kindness. Keep in mind that it is your behaviour and intentions that are important—and the feelings may follow on behind. Now bring to mind a time when you felt compassionate towards the person (or animal):

- Imagine yourself expanding as if you are becoming calmer, wiser, stronger and more mature, and able to help that person.
- Pay attention to your body as you remember your feelings of kindness. Create a compassionate facial expression.
- Spend a moment with any expansion and warmth in your body. Note a real genuine desire for this other person to be free of suffering and to flourish.
- Spend one minute, more if you are able, thinking about your tone of voice and the kind of things you said or the kind of things you did or wanted to do.
- Spend one minute, more if you are able, thinking about your pleasure in being able to be kind.

Now just focus on your desire to be helpful and kind, the sense of warmth, a feelings of expansion, your tone of voice, the wisdom in your voice and in your behaviour. When you have finished the exercise you might want to make some notes about how this felt for you.

Focusing the compassionate self on others

We can move on to focusing and directing our compassionate self. To practise this, find a time and place where you can sit quietly without being disturbed. Now try to create a sense of being a compassionate person, as best you can.

Some days this will be easier than others—even just the slightest glimmer can be a start. Now focus and bring to mind someone you care about (e.g., a partner, friend, parent or child) or an animal, or even a plant. When you have them in mind, focus on directing towards them three basic feelings and thoughts:

1   May you be well.
2   May you be happy.
3   May you be free of suffering.

Keep in mind that it is your behaviour and intentions that are important—and the feelings may follow on behind. Be gentle, take time and allow yourself to focus on desires and wishes you create in yourself for the other person/animal/plant. Maybe picture them smiling at you and sharing these feelings. Okay, that's tricky if you are thinking of a plant, but imagine the plant as "happy" to receive your compassionate wishes. Spend time focusing on this genuine desire of yours for "the other".

Remember to be mindful in the sense that if your mind wanders that is *not* a problem; just gently and kindly bring it back to your task. Try to notice any feelings you have in yourself and your body that emerge from this focusing exercise. Don't worry if nothing much happens at a conscious level—the act of having a go is the important thing. Like getting fit—it may take some visits to the gym or training before you consciously notice feeling different, but your body will be responding straight away.

There are many variations on this basic set of exercises including extending your imagery to others, strangers and even people you don't like. With all these exercises it is useful to help the client keep in mind that "all of us just find ourselves here with a brain and social conditioning that we didn't choose—all want happiness, none seek suffering". For more information on these kinds of exercises you can look at Germer (2009), Gilbert (2009a) and Ricard (2003).

Keep in mind all the time that these are behavioural experiments and you are collaborating and checking with the person how they feel, how useful it is to them, whether they see the point, whether there is anything they'd like to change, whether they have any ways that they would like to innovate—and so on. Go back to the three circles (page 43) and brain map (page 146).

From imagery to behaviour

In this short book we are focusing on imagery but keep in mind that compassionate behaviour is extremely important. There is now a lot of evidence that doing kind things for others helps us. So, you can also focus on compassionate behaviour, planning and thinking about how to practise and enact compassionate behaviour to others in between sessions. For example, do one *kind* act for self and someone else each day. Also, help people distinguish between "submissive niceness" or doing things because the client wants to be "nice" and liked (and we all do that to a degree), and genuine compassionate behaviour. Help people distinguish between what others want and what they need (e.g., an alcoholic wants another drink but that's not what they need). While helping, showing gratitude and appreciation can be compassionate, setting boundaries can also be compassionate behaviour. So, *not* buying that cream cake and being kind and understanding to the loss would be compassionate.

25

Compassion flowing into oneself: Using memory

Research on attention allocation has long shown that we are more attentive to threats than to positives (Baumeister et al., 2001). People are faster at finding aggressive faces in a matrix of happy or neutral faces than they are at finding a happy face in a matrix of neutral or negative faces (Öhman, Lundqvist, & Esteves, 2001). Beck has often pointed out that if we (say) go to ten shops and nine of the assistants are helpful but then one is rude and abusive the likelihood is that when we get home we will ruminate on the rude one and forget about the helpful ones. This is because our brain is set to be "threat sensitive more than reward sensitive" (Baumeister et al., 2001; Gilbert, 1998) and it becomes even more so when we're in stressed or threat brain-states. So, we need to work against this tendency, train in refocusing on the helpfulness of others, learning how to pay attention and "dwell" on the kindness of others—no matter how small. When I mentioned this to one of my borderline folk her response was, "F*** that; they're all bastards out there!" Nevertheless, doing simple out-of-session work of noticing kindnesses, no matter how small (e.g., the smile of a shop assistant) can be useful training; paying more attention to the content of our (threat or anger) ruminations and choosing to switch to kindness focusing (see Figure 4, page 65).

Building on this and trying to generate experiences of receiving compassion from others (interpersonal compassion), the next set of practices and exercises involve compassion flowing into oneself. Now this is where compassion work starts to get very tricky and you can run into various forms of resistance and fears, which are discussed in Point 29. It is useful to help people refocus their attention on times when other people were caring and helpful to them because these times are often forgotten or become less accessible when people feel threatened, angry or depressed. If we are angry with our partner we often don't stop and think about the things we like about them at the time we're angry. Indeed, the ability to switch to recall the positive qualities of the relationship (rather than ruminate on our dissatisfactions) is key to successful relating. So, people need to practice the experience and focus of compassion flowing into self. Here is some guidance for using memory—but keep in mind that some people may have very few such memories.

Guidance

Engage in your soothing rhythm breathing for a minute or so or until you can just feel your body slowing down. As you feel your body slowing down, prepare for your compassionate imagery by allowing your body posture to become compassionate. Feel it slightly expanding around you. Create your compassionate facial expression. This might involve a slight smile or relaxed posture, but it is a gentle facial expression. You may want to "play around" with facial expressions and see which one fits for you. When you feel ready, bring to mind a memory of a time when someone was kind to you.

This memory shouldn't be of a time when you were very distressed, because you will then focus on the distress. The point of the exercise is to focus on a desire to help and kindness. Create a compassionate expression on your face and a body posture that gives you the sense of kindness as you recall.

Spend one minute exploring the facial expressions of the person who was kind to you. Sometimes it helps if you see them moving towards you, or see their face breaking into a smile, or the head on one side. Focus on important sensory qualities of your memory in the following way:

- Just focus on the kinds of things this person said and the *tone* of their voice. Spend one minute on that.
- Then focus on the feeling of the emotion in the person, what they really felt for you at that moment. Focus on that for one minute (longer if you wish/can).
- Now focus on the whole experience, maybe whether they touched you or helped you in other ways, and notice your sense of gratitude and pleasure at being helped. Allow that experience of *gratitude* and *joy* in being helped to grow. Remember to keep your facial expression as compassionate as you can. Spend a few minutes with that memory. When you are ready, gently let the memory fade, come out of your exercise and make some notes on how you felt.

Contrasting memories

You may note that bringing these memories to mind may create feelings inside you even if they are just glimmers. To demonstrate this consider what would happen if you focused on how other people have been *un*kind to you? You would clearly create very different feelings inside yourself. The funny thing is that because we don't really pay attention to what goes on in our minds we can allow ourselves to exist (ruminate and dwell) in places where we recall (or anticipate) other people being unkind or threatening to us. That means we spend time stimulating our threat system. When we do that we block out more helpful memories and brain patterns. The question is: What do we want to train our minds for? Where do we want to exist in the patterns we can create in our minds? Where do we want to shine the spotlight of our consciousness?

You will notice that the focus on sensory qualities is important; get into the details of the imagery and the memory; holding these in mind is helpful. It is insufficient just to have a thought or cognition that others can be helpful. It is better to really allow the memory to stimulate affect systems by spending time with the memory. However, not all have such memories—or find this helpful—so always experiment and see what works for whom.

26

Compassion flowing into oneself: Compassionate images

The next exercises explore how people generate feelings of compassion flowing in. Again, this is an exercise that can run up against a lot of resistance (see Point 29), so it is useful to revisit the three circles diagram (page 43) and also the brain map (page 146) to clarify the importance of this exercise and working with resistance. You keep coming back to "physiotherapy for the mind" and trying to work around resistance.

This type of exercise has been used in many therapies (Frederick & McNeal, 1999) and spiritual traditions (Leighton, 2003). For example, Buddhists spend many hours meditating on the compassionate Buddha and feeling compassion flowing from the Buddha into the heart of the self. People who believe in God can imagine God loving them. Research has shown that even people who are atheists can still benefit from imagining being loved in this way (for a fascinating exploration with research findings, see Newberg & Waldman, 2007, especially Chapter 9).

In standard Buddhist practices the image of the Buddha is given to the person and must follow traditional sequences sometimes with chanting—a top-down approach. In our work we have a bottom-up approach where the person works to think about what would be compassionate for him or her. In our exercises people are asked to create and imagine *their ideal* compassion image. The act of thinking about what it is that would make *their ideal* compassionate image "*ideal for them*" is important for the exercise. It helps if they can think about what *they* really want from feeling compassion from another. Do they want protection, understanding, to be known fully,

185

validated, or to feel valued and just cared for? Are they fearful of any of these; are they contemptuous of any of these or do they just think it is impossible? As noted above, humans have evolved to seek out care from others (Hrdy, 2009) and to feel that others care about them (Gilbert, 1989, 2007a) and want the best for them. So that motivation (having deep concern and wishes for the person) arising in and from the compassionate image will be crucial.

In an early study of clients' own images of compassion Gilbert and Irons (2004) found that they easily understood the value of generating such images, and generated images that ranged from images of sunlight, a warm sea, an enfolding bush to those of Jesus. Feelings of "warmth", both physical and emotional, were commonly associated with the image. Individuals who have been neglected or abused often prefer non-human forms of an image to start with. However, over time images become more human-like. Some people feel barriers between themselves and their image because of issues of unresolved shame (e.g., the client may be having sexual or aggressive fantasies that they can't reveal—but their image could know; Mayhew & Gilbert, 2008). Sometimes the barriers are related to fear that the image will suddenly become critical or rejecting or hurtful—or just not be there when needed (often linked to memories of childhood).

It can help (but not always) if they imagine that their compassionate image was at one time like them, and hence struggled with all the same things that they have, but has now moved on. They understand the person's problems from the inside and not just as some distant "spiritual, up on a cloud" perspective. Here again we are tapping into the psychology of "mind sharing" (Gilbert, 2007a; Hrdy, 2009; Stern, 2004).

When people do these exercises it is common to have thoughts about "not deserving" or that they can't do it, or it may even feel a bit frightening. Or you get Groucho Marx-type thoughts, "I would not want compassion for someone who had compassion for someone like me!" The threat system can be active and at first can block these "compassion for self" feelings (see Point 29). Don't worry about that, it's typical with high-shame folk. Advise that, "To the best of your ability just prac-tise the exercise in any way you can and see what happens. You would not say to yourself that you didn't deserve to be fit, or if you want to play the piano that you didn't deserve to play the piano. Keep this in mind when you are thinking about training your mind. Even if you feel nothing is happening the act of practising and trying is moving you forward".

Creating an "ideal and a perfect" compassionate image for the self

In this imagery work I have taken key qualities from what Buddhists call Bodhisattvas. These are beings who at one time were human but have become enlightened and wise and are now fully and totally dedicated by compassion to relieve the suffering of all beings (Leighton, 2003; Vessantara, 1993). So, below are secular exercises designed to stimulate certain brain areas—upon which we await more research (but see Ji-Woong et al., 2009; Lutz et al., 2008).

Now, there are many ways to start this exercise. You can go straight into it if your client prefers, but here is a way that some prefer. Spend time meditating on each quality (e.g., commit-ment, wisdom for self, etc.) and what each feels like to receive.

Guidance

First, engage with your soothing breathing rhythm and compassionate expression; bring to mind your safe place, the sounds, the feel, and the sights. Remind yourself that this is your place and it delights in your being there. This may now be the place where you wish to create and meet your com-passionate image. You can imagine your image being created out of a mist in front of you, for example. The image may be walking towards you. (Note: *In Buddhist practice the student imagines a clear blue sky from which various images emerge.*)

This exercise is to help you *build up* a compassionate image, for you to work with and develop (you can have more than one if you wish, and they can change over time). Whatever image comes to mind or you choose to work with, note that it *is your* creation and therefore your own personal ideal—what you would really like from feeling cared for/about. However, in this practice it is important that you try to give your image certain qualities (outlined below). These are superhuman—complete and perfect compassionate qualities that never let you down. So, if your image ever seems disappointed or critical, or not completely warm, or lacks authority and strength—then refocus on creating those qualities. Remember that this work is to help stimulate brain areas for you and so practising these "pure, perfect qualities of compassion" in our imagination is key. These qualities include:

- *A deep commitment* to you—a desire to help you heal, cope with and relieve your suffering, and take more joy from your life. (*Note*: This focusing on experiences of care intentions from another is key from the evolutionary point of view.)
- *Wisdom*—which comes from three sources. First, it understands that "we all just find ourselves here" having to cope with a brain we did not design and early life experiences that shaped us that we did not choose. Second, it understands our own personal life history and why we use the safety strategies we do. Third, at one time it has lived through many life experiences of its own and so it is not some separate mind that has little idea of human struggles. It has gained through experience—it truly understands the struggles we go through in life. We all "just find ourselves here" doing the best we can.
- *Strength of mind*—it is not overwhelmed by your pain or distress, but remains present, enduring it with you. It has

confidence and authority derived in part from its wisdom.
- *Warmth*—conveyed by kindness, gentleness, caring and openness.
- *Acceptance*—it is never judgemental or critical, it understands your struggles and accepts you as you are. However, remember, too, that it is deeply committed to help you and support you.

Please don't worry about remembering all of these qualities and emotions because you will be guided through them again when we do the imagery.

We also stress the importance of "the wish" intention and effort so that clients don't get hung up on trying to create emotions of warmth, when in fact they may be quite a long time developing; especially if feelings in general are problematic for them (see Point 4). So, it is the desire, the focus, the intention, the wish to experience these things that's important, often with feelings coming later.

As mentioned, the compassionate image has a deep commitment and desire to enhance the well-being of the client. This means that it will have preferences for the client. So, for example, if the client is wanting to give up smoking or drinking, the compassionate image will desire that for the person and the client can then focus on experiencing their compassionate image wanting them to be free of the smoking or drinking—but never condemning setbacks. Clearly, the image is to promote well-being and not just any goals—for example, it would not be supportive of anorexic goals, or suicidal escape—though of course understanding. For very complex clients these can be difficult dialogues, and some images can seem very uncompassionate (Mayhew & Gilbert, 2008).

Although these qualities are clearly those of the human mind, the compassion image may not take human form. Our early studies suggested that often it doesn't and people have compassionate images of a tree, an animal or the sun or even a mountain (Gilbert & Irons, 2004, 2005). The actual form an image takes may not be important as long as the person experiences it as having this type of compassionate mind with compassionate motives directed to the self.

Sometimes it helps for people to work on the sensory qualities of the image and sometimes it doesn't. In the early days of CFT we did spend more time on the visual aspects of an image as this can be difficult for people. In spiritual traditions people are often given an image. Nonetheless, if the sensory imagery is useful to your client you can offer a variety of forms for writing down the exercises (see Gilbert, 2009a, 2009b). Here is a simple one:

Recoding your imagery work

How would you like your ideal caring-compassionate image to look/appear—visual qualities?
How would you like your ideal caring-compassionate image to sound (e.g., voice tone)?
What other sensory qualities can you give to it?
How would you like your ideal caring-compassionate image to relate to you?
How would like to relate to your ideal caring-compassionate image?

In each box clients can think of these qualities (wisdom, strength, warmth and non-judgement, see Point 16) and imagine what they would look, sound or feel like. If nothing comes to mind, or the mind wanders, they can *gently* just bring it back to the breathing and practise compassionately accepting this.

Here are some questions that might help people build an image:

- Would you want your caring/nurturing image to feel/look/seem old or young; to be male or female (or non-human looking, e.g., an animal, sea or light)?
- What colours and sounds are associated with the qualities of wisdom, strength, warmth and non-judgement?
- What would help you sense their commitment and kindness for you?

One of the key experiences is that their image *really wants* for them to be free of suffering, and/or to be able to deal with the difficulties, and to flourish. It knows that we all just find ourselves here, living as we do, trying to make the best of our minds and lives. It understands that our minds are difficult, that emotions can run riot in us and this is not our fault.

Guidance

Practise experiencing what it's like to focus on the feeling that another mind really values you and cares about you unconditionally. Now focus on the idea that your compassionate ideal is looking at you with great warmth. Imagine that they have the following deep desires for you:

- that you be well;
- that you be happy;
- that you be free of suffering.

The key to the exercise *is not* the visual clarity. Indeed, some people don't really see their images in any clear way at all. The key to the exercise is to focus and practise on the compassionate desires coming into you. Here the practice is to imagine another mind wishing for you to flourish.

Now, you might have thought, "Yes but this is not real, I want somebody real to care for me". That is, of course, very understandable and even doing this exercise could make you feel sad. That is because your intuitive wisdom recognizes seeking for connectedness. The point to remember is that what we are trying to tackle is your own attitudes towards yourself, particularly feelings of shame or self-criticism. While it may indeed be desirable to find people who are caring, it's also very desirable that you create these feelings within you—so that you gradually learn to focus on compassion for yourself, rather than self-criticism. So, try not to see it as an "either/or" situation, but as quite different processes between the compassion you give to yourself, and the compassion you'd like other people to give to you.

Being understood and known

People can imagine that their compassionate image understands the difficulty and complexity of being a human being and their current lives and experiences. There is nothing that they can feel, do or imagine that another human hasn't done at some point. That's because these are related to our brain design. A compassionate image knows that we are working with a brain that we didn't design. It has gained wisdom and understanding from experience, therefore can perfectly understand and fully accept the person—and wants them to be free from suffering and to flourish.

This is important because sometimes we have thoughts like, "Sure, but if my compassionate image knew this or that about me, knew about my bad feelings, fantasies or thoughts or things that I've done, then maybe it wouldn't be compassionate". We explain that compassion is not a "fair weather friend". Compassion matters at the point of suffering, at the point of difficulty. Compassion to just nice things is not really compassion! This often opens up issues of forgiveness—for which there is now a large literature—and although this is part of CFT, space does not allow for a detailed exploration here.

From imagery to behaviour

As noted above, although we are focusing on imagery we also teach people self-compassionate behaviour. This is not so much about "doing nice things for the self" such as taking a bath or going out for a meal (though it could be). Compassionate behaviour is really about what we need to do to flourish and sometimes that means confronting complex and difficult situations. So, it can be helpful for therapist and client together to generate ideas for compassionate behaviour to be acted on and practised over the week. When clients really understand that grappling with difficulty can be done in the spirit of compassion it can help their motivation. One client recognized that she needed to leave a relationship and the most compassionate thing she could do for herself was to tackle that issue, and cope with guilt. In ACT terms compassion aids commitment.

27

Compassionate letter writing

This is a form of expressive writing—for which there is now good evidence of usefulness (Pennebaker, 1997). Writing to oneself helps people assimilate difficult experiences and can be used in many ways. When writing a letter to themselves from a compassionate point of view, the client can imagine hearing the voice of their compassionate image talking to them and they write that down, or they can put themselves into the compassionate-self mode and write from that position, or they can imagine a friend writing to them, or what they would like to say to a friend. Again, engage in behavioural experiments. Do this in the spirit of finding the tone that is helpful to that person. You can leave the room for a few minutes so people have some space to write "in session" or do it as out of session work. You can then read out their letters to them in a gentle voice, or invite them to read to you and see the tones they use. You can also use this as a training vehicle because to begin with clients may not write very compassionate letters, and part of your skill is to recognize this and shape their writing and focus.

Is the letter:

- expressive of concern and genuine caring?
- sensitive to the person's distress and needs?
- sympathetic and emotionally moved by their distress?
- helpful in facing and becoming more mindful and tolerant of their feelings?
- helpful in becoming more understanding and reflective of their feelings, difficulties and dilemmas?
- non-judgemental/condemning?
- permeated with a genuine sense of warmth, understanding and caring?

- helpful in thinking about the behaviour they may need to attempt in order to move forward?

The point of these letters is *not* just to focus on difficult feelings but also to help people stand back and reflect empathically on and be open with feelings and thoughts, and to develop compassionate and balanced ways of working with them. They will not offer "advice" or "I shoulds", etc. For more information on letter writing see Gilbert (2009a, 2009b).

28

Compassion and well-being enhancing

Stimulated by Martin Seligman's concept of positive psychology on strengths and virtues (Peterson & Seligman, 2004), clinicians have become more aware that we need to help people, not just by working with their threats and problematic behaviours, but also by helping them develop well-being. This positive approach is increasingly being integrated into various therapies (Synder & Ingram, 2006). We now know that well-being is linked to a range of elements such as a sense of purpose and control in one's life, feeling that one can make a difference for others, feeling gratitude and the ability to appreciate other people and the small pleasures of life. If science continues to show that one of the most important components of well-being is the ability to love and be loved, to care and to be caring, then our psychological therapies, interventions and training will become increasingly focused on that, be this in our clinics, schools or workplaces.

So, compassion is also a way of thinking about enhance-ments and this means, again, recognizing the *attributes* of well-being and personal enhancements that are socially contextua-lized and responsive, and *the skills*. Figure 12 provides a simple model. First, we are motivated to working for our and others' well-being, and to be open to caring and finding contentment. We are able to think about our needs, which, in the long term, will sustain and flourish us, and distinguish those from our wants. The alcoholic wants another drink but that's not what he/she needs. We might want more money but that won't necessarily train our brains for well-being. We can learn to appreciate things rather than becoming quickly used to them and then bored and desirous of more. Even lottery winners go back to feeling their typical moods after a few months.

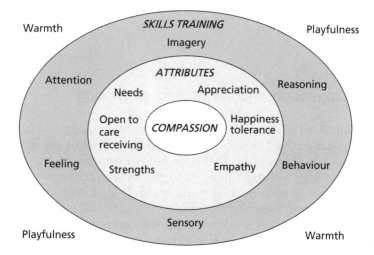

Figure 12 Multimodal compassionate mind training (CMT) for positive and affiliative enhancement

For some people happiness tolerance is important. As noted in Point 29, there can be major fears of happiness and positive emotions. We need to have empathy and understanding about well-being and the importance of focusing on well-being. Finally, it's learning to play to our strengths within a compassionate framework. Being a good sniper or conman might be a strength, but not one we would recommend.

Helping people think about personal and social enhancements, and not just treating them as "psychiatric cases", is very important. Remember that we can only be one version of ourselves, but that other versions are always possible—we train for them. All of these approaches are helping us to widen and build our therapeutic efforts.

29

Fear of compassion

When people are depressed they often feel unmotivated to do positive things, even though (they know) those things might help them. Anxious people might love to do certain things such as fly away on holiday, go on a new date, take exciting jobs but are too fearful to try. Arousal and the threat–self-protection system blocks activities that could lead to positive feelings and self-enhancement. There can be a fear of doing things even though people anticipate that they would have positive feelings and grow from doing them. In these contexts encouraging engagement and activity in depressed people, or helping the anxious person tolerate and work with anxious feelings, is helpful.

What has been less researched but is becoming increasingly clear within Compassion Focused Therapy is *the fear of positive emotion itself*. To understand this, one must keep clear the two types of positive emotion (see Point 6). In fact, people can have the fear of both. Thirty years ago Arieti and Bemporad (1980) argued that some depressed people have a taboo on pleasure. They have grown up in puritanical environments, believing that pleasure is somehow bad. Indeed, people can have beliefs that if they are happy today something bad will happen tomorrow. Sometimes this is linked to emotional memory and conditioning where an individual was happy and then something bad happened. For example, Susan recalls looking forward to things such as a birthday party, but then her mother would often become upset or angry, creating a bad atmosphere. Or they would plan to go out to the seaside but, as an agoraphobic, her mother would suddenly have a panic and so "all coats were taken off and dad would get angry". So, "I feel

199

uneasy if I start to feel happy", she said. Some people believe that "happiness is just not part of me". They have an identity that is locked into suffering and depression and can't imagine themselves being happy. Some people hold on to their "victim-hood" as an identity, to be taken out and polished for anyone who will listen. For some it is anger that holds it all in place. People with OCD sometimes notice their symptoms worsening when feeling happy as well as when stressed.

Compassion, however, is a particular kind of positive affect that is linked to social relationships and feelings of content-ment, safeness and connectedness. For some people the positive feelings, generated by endorphins and oxytocin, of loving and feeling content are extremely frightening. This is because these types of positive feelings require one to open up to others to some extent, and to become more trusting and to recognize that one can survive the ups and downs of relationships. We "lower our guard". The problem is the closing down of this affect system and thus knocking out the most important soothing system in our brain! Indeed, some children and adults have learnt that they need to isolate themselves to feel safe; to turn away from others not towards them when distressed. This can be a key problem in engaging people with complex mental-health problems with appropriate services of course.

Many years ago attachment theorist John Bowlby noted in an interview that if he was nice to clients they would sometimes become irritable, anxious or simply not come back. He realized that kindness was opening the attachment system. The problem is that if there are aversive memories of attachment figures "in the system" these can be triggered by the kindness of the therapist. This is shown in Figure 13.

Some evidence

In my research unit, Rockliff et al. (2008) explored a measure of emotional processing called Heart Rate Variability (HRV). This study revealed that low self-critics responded to compassion

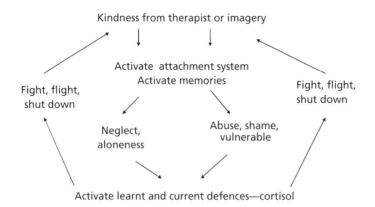

Figure 13 Ways kindness and compassion can relate to attachment, threat and avoidance. Reproduced with kind permission from Gilbert, P. (2009c) "Evolved minds and compassion-focused imagery in depression", in L. Stopa (ed.), *Imagery and the Threatened Self: Perspectives on Mental Imagery and the Self in Cognitive Therapy* (pp. 206–231). London: Routledge

imagery with an increase in HRV and reduction in cortisol, indicating that it was a soothing experience, whereas high self-criticism was associated with a reduction in HRV (indicating threat) and no change in cortisol. Longe et al. (2010) used fMRI to investigate neurophysiological responses to self-criticism and self-reassurance in the context of a distressing event (e.g., getting a job rejection). Not only were there clear neurophysiological differences between self-reassuring and self-critical responses, but those higher in self-criticism seemed to show a threat-like pattern when trying to be self-reassuring and compassionate—a finding similar to Rockliff et al. (2008). Psychotherapy has to work on that compassion-as-threat difficulty, otherwise self-critics are not able to access an important soothing system, and this may impact on relapse vulnerability. There are several reasons why compassion can be threatening.

Conditioning

CFT is very linked with classical conditioning models and we can use classical conditioning to understand this problem. For example, our own sex feelings are pleasurable, but if we were (say) raped they would become aversive. What are normally pleasurable *internal* motives, feelings and activities can become highly aversive. Understanding the *fear and unpleasantness* in experiencing warm feelings is exactly the same. Normally feelings of others being kind or helpful are pleasant, but if it stimulates a desire for closeness, which reminds you of abuse and being out of control, overwhelmed, obligated, fearfully dependent or smothered, then those are not pleasant emotions. Sometimes, because parents are both wanted and feared (Liotti, 2000), this is what reappears in compassion work. So, one reason that the soothing system is problematic is that it has a lot of toxic and threat-focused memories and conditioned emotional reactions associated with it. Sometimes just feelings of warmth can stimulate a whole range of unprocessed and difficult emotions and memories.

Grieving

A common problem for people on their route to compassion is that it awakens in them social mentalities for wanting to feel safe through being cared for, wanted and a sense of belonging (Baumeister & Leary, 1995). However, this recognition of wanting to feel loved and connected can overwhelm them with feelings of sadness. We explain this (and their tears) as "an intuitive wisdom" because yearning to connect is how our brains have evolved and the way we are designed. Grief can be the beginning of a recognition of yearning for connectedness, and processing feelings of deep loss and failed efforts to feel loved and wanted from childhood (Bowlby, 1980). Although there have been many studies looking at specific losses in childhood (bereavements), such as the loss of a parent or loss due to illness, there are very few studies looking at loss of what was wanted or needed. This is the loss of a desired childhood because of (say) abuse. The ability to grieve for what did not happen (e.g., feeling loved and wanted), as well as what did (e.g., abuse), is important. Gilbert and Irons (2005) suggested that borderline personality difficulties are especially associated with difficulties tolerating grief and sadness for what are often immense loss-filled lives.

So, CFT does grief work (which is a form of behaviour tolerance of sadness and yearning). A well-known CBT therapist once told me that grief for the past was unhelpful to therapy and to be avoided. In CFT it can be essential. Although we lack good evidence, many of the borderline folk we have worked with (e.g., Gilbert & Procter, 2006) have felt that being given space to grieve for the traumas of childhood and the yearning for love and protection were major steps in recovery. For people who suffer injuries, or major illnesses, or run into a psychosis, space to grieve can be an important part of the recovery process. However, early on this can be so overwhelming that they might dissociate from it.

Nonetheless, gentle, collaborative persistence can pay off. One of my clients, who had spent months working through terrible grief for her background, became aware that she had started to have all kinds of feelings that she never knew existed. Before grieving, her emotions seemed frozen without her really realizing it. So, just as blocked grief for the loss of a loved one can cause psychological problems more research is needed on the process of grieving for the hardships of one's own life. Clearly there are times when grieving is not helpful, tears are related to frustrated "poor me", or people just perseverate. Nonetheless, grief can be treated like any other emotion where toleration and working with and through it is key. This is more difficult to do in group therapy and it helps if individuals have personal therapists (as in DBT) who understand its processes. Some aspects of grieving may be linked to "distress calling" and when individuals begin to experience others as present, available and helpful this resets the affect-regulation systems and reduces threat-based impulsivity. On that matter, though, far more research is needed—but certainly there are many anecdotal stories that when people feel loved, wanted and accepted (e.g., even in finding a religion) it "changes them". It is extraordinary that so little research has been focused on these aspects and the implications for psychotherapy.

Metacognition

Fear of compassion can also be associated with various meta-cognitions (see Point 4). People can believe it's a self-indulgence; it will make them weak; they don't deserve it; it'll be okay today but will change tomorrow. Currently we are undertaking studies on the fear of compassion. This is related to fear of being compassionate to others, fear of accepting and being open to compassion from others and fear of being compassionate to oneself. Current data suggest that all of these three are related to stress, anxiety and depression, with fear of self-compassion particularly correlated.

In a qualitative study of self-compassion in depression Pauley and McPherson (in press) found that most people had not ever considered being self-compassionate (a finding similar to Gilbert & Procter, 2006). However, they felt that although learning to be self-compassionate would be extremely helpful they also felt that it would be extremely difficult because their sense of self was locked into self-criticism, especially when depressed. Some participants thought that it would create too big a change in self-identity, and that depression itself creates inner self-dislike that is difficult to counteract. Developing better understanding and further research on the complex blocks, barriers and resistances to developing self-compassion is therefore urgently required. Indeed, in therapy it requires careful elicitation, analysis and collaborative agreements to work on those barriers.

Lack of feeling

Another common problem is that when people begin to do their imagery and compassion work they just can't get any "warm or compassionate feelings". One client said, "It all feels pretty dead in there—absolutely no feeling". For these individuals it's useful to suggest that this is not surprising given their background, and the fact that their affiliative-soothing systems may not have had the chance to develop, or might be under threat control, or might be knocked out because of the brain state of depression itself. The key thing, though, is to do the practice, and focus on the desires, motives and intentions to try compassionate focusing. Feelings can come and go, and although we hope that more "soothing" feeling will come through, it can take a lot of time and practice.

Developmental difficulties

Point 4 explored the importance of developmental competencies, particularly those associated with mentalizing and the abilities to think about, describe and reflect on one's emotions. If people are struggling here—perhaps with mentalizing problems or alexithymic difficulties—compassionate feelings are going to be very strange to them, simply because they can't articulate, or can hardly discriminate, *any* feelings. So, compassion work here can be very slow, with a lot of focus on in-therapy feelings and specific exercises. These individuals also closely monitor their *in*ability to feel or describe feelings, have preset ideas of what certain feelings should be like, and become self-critical (ashamed) very quickly. That immediately switches them into the threat system and the whole endeavour collapses. In my view part of the problem with alexithymia is that people become ashamed or self-critical of the explorative process itself. They have thoughts like: "This should be easy; I should know this; I should be able to do this; What's the matter with me; I feel silly sitting here trying to talk about feelings I don't feel or understand". At other times certain types of emotion can emerge (like grieving or rage) but are felt as overwhelming and therefore people engage in avoidance. So, teaching how to tolerate and explore emotion, allowing and just noticing the self-critical content, can be a beginning process. Emotional recognition and working through is also an area addressed within emotion focused therapy (e.g., Greenberg et al., 1993) and some of the newer mentalizing approaches (Bateman & Fonagy, 2006).

Playfulness

In CFT, therapists *constantly try to create a "sense of safeness"* and engagement that facilitates exploration. Because CFT started out with very highly shame-prone, self-critical people it has always been very focused on this issue—of how easy shame and self-criticism are to trigger and how important constantly shifting out of the threat system and into the soothing system is—and the hard work that involves.

Safeness creates the (neurophysiological) conditions for exploration and developmental change. This exploration can be of things that have happened or are happening in the outside world but also of one's inner world and state. In childhood, learning is best conducted under conditions of playfulness and low threat. The same is true in therapy. We have *greatly* under-estimated the importance of playfulness in terms of creating emotional contexts that facilitate exploration and are de-shaming. In CFT playfulness is a very important therapeutic ingredient where the therapist has gentleness with encourage-ment to explore. Playfulness can help clients feel safe. If one thinks of compassionate individuals, those who are easy to be with, a sense of playfulness is very strongly represented—yet also the ability to become focused with intent too. Playfulness also depends on the non-verbal communicative styles of the therapist. In CFT playfulness is also linked to threat within the therapist (e.g., from having to meet targets!).

For individuals who struggle with compassion, maybe have problems mentalizing, then engaging gently and playfully can be important first steps. Christine Braehler (December 2009, personal communication), who has just completed a series of compassion focused groups with people with psychosis, has noted how the group became compassionate to each other and playful around certain themes and ideas—able to share a joke. She noted how important that was for facilitating the group process. We are a very long way away from those encounter groups of the 1960s!

Desensitization

In many ways you're working with standard behavioural interventions based on desensitization; helping people tolerate and feel things that they may be avoiding. In addition, you're creating conditions through your compassion focused therapeutic relationship, developing the client's own compassionate self, compassionate chair work, compassionate letter writing and imagery, and abilities to facilitate compassionate feeling and understanding.

Function analysis

It is useful to articulate the fear of compassion as understandable and then explore it from a functional-analysis point of view. What are the greatest fears/threats of developing compassion? What are the key blocks? If one visualizes oneself as a compassionate person in the future, what problems are associated with that? To proceed with a therapy that aims to activate a particular evolved emotional system does of course require close collaboration with the clients because it may involve them beginning to feel things they have avoided. So, rather than thinking of avoidance in terms of specific emotions, we can think about it in terms of specific emotion *systems*. As noted above there is still much to learn about the blocks and fears of compassion. It is often the blocks and fears that *is the central work*.

30

Last thoughts

This book has outlined the basic model of CFT. It is a science-based and multi-focused approach as opposed to a "school of therapy"-based model. It is not a Buddhist model, although it clearly values and utilizes Buddhist insights and teachings. Germer (2009) gives an excellent overview of a more Buddhist approach, blending mindfulness with a number of compassion focused exercises. This is written as a self-help book and can therefore be recommended to clients. CFT is rooted in evolutionary theory, the neuroscience of affect regulation, the way new and older brain systems interact (such as with mentalizing and theory of mind competencies) and the qualities of (social) relationships. It utilizes findings from developmental, social and other branches of psychology and it is closely aligned with many behavioural concepts such as emotional conditioning. So, CFT seeks to recruit and integrate knowledge from the scientific study of psychology and develop therapies from that position rather than any "specific school of therapy" approach.

In terms of interventions (e.g., Figure 1, page 25) CFT is a multimodal therapy, that builds on the significant and important advances of ACT, CBT, DBT, EFT, REBT and many other approaches. Compassion focused therapists check carefully that whatever intervention they use (be it via the therapeutic relationship, helping people re-examine their thoughts or core beliefs, operating against safety behaviours, acknowledging and working with anger or traumatic memories, engaging exposure to what is feared, behavioural experiments or graded tasks, work with body focused sensations/feelings, or developing mindfulness) the person is able to do these in the spirit of validation, support and kindness, rather than with an underlying inner affect of detachment, invalidation, coldness, bullying or criticalness. The motivational and emotional tone, the basic orientation, intention and the spirit of the intervention *is key*. So, too, is developing self-compassion; this is not only a way of approaching cognitive, behavioural and emotion-based interventions but also of building a self-identity that is able to practise "becoming the compassionate self". As noted, there are many anecdotal stories that when people feel loved, wanted and accepted (e.g., even in finding a religion) it "changes them". It is extraordinary that outside the attachment focused psychotherapists, so little research has been focused on the implications (interventions) for CBT—given that we have evolved to be care seekers (Gilbert, 1989, 2007a; Hrdy, 2009) with strong needs for a sense of belonging and feeling valued (Baumeister & Leary, 1995).

CFT also stresses a developmental approach to change. People go through stages of change relating to motivation but also psychological competencies (such as abilities to mentalize and various cognitive capacities for abstract thinking). So, people can begin to recognize that they have problems with their emotions but simply feel a victim to them. At the next stage they begin to recognize these are things happening within "their minds" and start to take a step back into a more observant role. However, they still feel that their emotions rule them. Later, people begin to recognize that they don't need to act out their feelings and that thoughts and feelings are not necessarily accurate reflections of reality—they are becoming more mindful and with mentalizing abilities. With this comes the ability to understand complex, and at times, conflicting emotions; that we have different parts of self with different priorities and motives. Awareness of this developmental process is important because one's therapy will vary according to where clients are in their cognitive, observant-mindfulness mentalizing and affect complexity abilities. However, in CFT, running through all these processes of change is also a process of becoming self-compassionate and stimulating specific types of affect-regulation systems in the brain. Indeed, the harnessing of inner compassion creates the conditions that facilitate feelings of safeness and soothing (undercuts self-criticism) and facilitates explorative behaviour, which in turn facilitates cognitive and affect maturation and mentalizing.

CFT focuses on the multiplicity of our minds, in that we have many different "parts of self" and can feel many different and, at times, conflicting motives and emotions towards particular events. Thus, identifying specific thoughts can be difficult or even misleading. Moreover, some emotions cloud and suppress others. Hence, the therapist helps the person slow down and draws out (using Socratic dialogues, guided discovery and empathy) a variety of the potential feelings and motives that could be aroused in a specific experience, including those that clients might avoid or be frightened to feel or acknowledge. We then of course stand back and view these difficult conflicts with normalising and compassion and reflect on which aspects to work with in a step-by-step way.

Although CFT is now being used for a range of psychological difficulties it was originally designed for people with high levels of shame and self-criticism, who found compassionate self-soothing very difficult. As we go to press various randomised controlled trials (RCTs) are being planned.

Most therapies now are increasingly building on a science of mind. This will mean they will naturally become more similar over time and (hopefully) less tribal. For me, the science is clear—we are an evolved species that functions best in conditions of safeness, support, connectedness and kindness.

So, may your compassionate practice serve you well.

References

Allen, J. H., Fonagy, P. and Bateman, A. W. (2008) *Mentalizing in Clinical Practice*. Washington, DC: American Psychiatric Association.

Allione, T. (2008) *Feeding Your Demons*. New York: Little Brown & Co.

Andrews, B. (1998) "Shame and childhood abuse", in P. Gilbert and B. Andrews (eds), *Shame: Interpersonal Behavior, Psychopathology and Culture* (pp. 176–190). New York: Oxford University Press.

Ardelt, M. (2003) "Empirical assessment of a three-dimensional wisdom scale", *Research on Aging*, 25: 275–324.

Arieti, S. and Bemporad, J. (1980) *Severe and Mild Depression: The Psychotherapeutic Approach*. London: Tavistock.

Baldwin, M. W. (ed.) (2005) *Interpersonal Cognition*. New York: Guilford Press.

Barkow, J. H. (1989) *Darwin, Sex and Status*. Toronto, Canada: Toronto University Press.

Bateman, A. and Fonagy, P. (2006) *Mentalizing-Based Treatment for Borderline Personality Disorder: A Practical Guide*. Oxford, UK: Oxford University Press.

Bates, A. (2005) "The expression of compassion in group cognitive therapy", in P. Gilbert (ed.), *Compassion: Conceptualisations, Research and Use in Psychotherapy* (pp. 379–386). London: Routledge.

Baumeister, R. F., Bratslavsky, E., Finkenauer, C. and Vohs, K. D.

(2001) "Bad is stronger than good", *Review of General Psychology*, 5: 323–370.

Baumeister, R. F. and Leary, M. R. (1995) "The need to belong: Desire for interpersonal attachments as a fundamental human motivation", *Psychological Bulletin*, 117: 497–529.

Baumeister, R. F., Stillwell, A. and Heatherton, T. F. (1994) "Guilt: An interpersonal approach", *Psychological Bulletin*, 115: 243–267.

Beck, A. T. (1987) "Cognitive models of depression", *Journal of Cognitive Psychotherapy: An International Quarterly*, 1: 5–38.

Beck, A. T. (1996) "Beyond belief: A theory of modes, personality and psychopathology", in P. Salkovskis (ed.), *Frontiers of Cognitive Therapy* (pp. 1–25). New York: Oxford University Press.

Beck, A. T., Emery, G. and Greenberg, R. L. (1985) *Anxiety Disorders and Phobias: A Cognitive Approach*. New York: Basic Books.

Beck, A. T., Freeman, A., Davis, D. D. and associates (2003) *Cognitive Therapy of Personality Disorders*, 2nd edn. New York: Guilford Press.

Begley, S. (2007) *Train your Mind, Change your Brain*. New York: Ballantine Books.

Bell, D. C. (2001) "Evolution of care giving behavior", *Personality and Social Psychology Review*, 5: 216–229.

Bennett-Levy, J. and Thwaites, R. (2007) "Self and self reflection in the therapeutic relationship", in P. Gilbert and R. Leahy (eds), *The Therapeutic Relationship in the Cognitive Behavioural Psychotherapies* (pp. 255–281). London: Routledge.

Bering, J. M. (2002) "The existential theory of mind", *Review of General Psychology*, 6: 3–34.

Bifulco, A. and Moran, P. (1998) *Wednesday's Child: Research into Women's Experiences of Neglect and Abuse in Childhood, and Adult Depression*. London: Routledge.

Black, S., Hardy, G., Turpin, G. and Parry, G. (2005) "Self-reported attachment styles and therapeutic orientation of therapists and their relationship with reported general alliance quality and problems in therapy", *Psychology and Psychotherapy*, 78: 363–377.

Blackmore, S. (1996) *The Meme Machine*. Oxford, UK: Oxford University Press.

Bowlby, J. (1969) *Attachment and Loss. Vol. 1: Attachment*. London: Hogarth Press.

Bowlby, J. (1973) *Attachment and Loss. Vol. 2: Separation, Anxiety and Anger*. London: Hogarth Press.

Bowlby, J. (1980) *Attachment and Loss. Vol. 3: Loss, Sadness and Depression*. London: Hogarth Press.

Brewin, C. R. (2006) "Understanding cognitive behaviour therapy: A retrieval competition account", *Behaviour Research and Therapy*, 44: 765–784.

Brewin, C. R., Wheatley, J., Patel, T., Fearon, P., Hackmann, A., Wells, A., et al. (2009) "Imagery rescripting as a brief stand-alone treatment for depressed patients with intrusive memories", *Behaviour Research and Therapy*, 47: 569–576.

Buss, D. M. (2003) *Evolutionary Psychology: The New Science of Mind*, 2nd edn. Boston: Allyn & Bacon.

Buss, D. M. (2009) "The great struggles of life: Darwin and the emergence of evolutionary psychology", *American Psychologist*, 64: 140–148.

Cacioppo, J. T., Berston, G. G., Sheridan, J. F. and McClintock, M. K. (2000) "Multilevel integrative analysis of human behavior: Social neuroscience and the complementing nature of social and biological approaches", *Psychological Bulletin*, 126: 829–843.

Carter, C. S. (1998) "Neuroendocrine perspectives on social attachment and love", *Psychoneuroendocrinology*, 23: 779–818.

Caspi, A. and Moffitt, T. E. (2006) "Gene–environment interactions in psychiatry: Joining forces with neuroscience", *Nature Reviews: Neuroscience*, 7: 583–590.

Choi-Kain, L. W. and Gunderson, J. G. (2008) "Mentalization: Ontogeny, assessment, and application in the treatment of border-line personality disorder", *American Journal of Psychiatry*, 165: 1127–1135.

Cooley, C. (1922) *Human Nature and the Social Order*, rev. edn. New York: Charles Scribner's Sons (originally published 1902).

Coon, D. (1992) *Introduction to Psychology: Exploration and Application*, 6th edn. New York: West Publishing Company.

Cozolino, L. (2007) *The Neuroscience of Human Relationships: Attachment and the Developing Brain*. New York: Norton.

Cozolino, L. (2008) *The Healthy Aging Brain: Sustaining Attachment, Attaining Wisdom*. New York: Norton.

Crane, R. (2009) *Mindfulness-Based Cognitive Therapy: Distinctive Features*. London: Routledge.

Crisp, R. J. and Turner, R. N. (2009) "Can imagined interactions produce positive perceptions? *American Psychologist*, 64: 231–240.

Crocker, J. and Canevello, A. (2008) "Creating and undermining social support in communal relationships: The role of compassionate and self-image goals", *Journal of Personality and Social Psychology*, 95: 555–575.

Cullen, C. and Combes, H. (2006) "Formulation from the perspective of contextualism", in N. Tarrier (ed.), *Case Formulation in Cognitive*

Behaviour Therapy: The Treatment of Challenging and Complex Cases (pp. 36–51). London: Routledge.

Dadds, M. R., Bovbjerg, D. H., Redd, W. H. and Cutmore, T. R. (1997) "Imagery in human classical conditioning", *Psychological Medicine*, 122: 89–103.

Dalai Lama (1995) *The Power of Compassion*. India: HarperCollins.

Darwin, C. (1859) *On the Origin of Species by Means of Natural Selection*. London: John Murray.

Davidson, R. J., Kabat-Zinn, J., Schumacher, J., Rosenkranz, M., Muller, D., Santorelli, S., et al. (2003) "Alterations in brain and immune function produced by mindfulness meditation", *Psychosomatic Medicine*, 65: 564–570.

Decety, J. and Jackson, P. L. (2004) "The functional architecture of human empathy", *Behavioral and Cognitive Neuroscience Reviews*, 3: 71–100.

Depue, R. A. and Morrone-Strupinsky, J. V. (2005) "A neurobehavioral model of affiliative bonding", *Behavioral and Brain Sciences*, 28: 313–395.

Didonna, F. (ed.) (2009) *Clinical Handbook of Mindfulness*. New York: Springer.

Dixon, A. K. (1998) "Ethological strategies for defence in animals and humans: Their role in some psychiatric disorders", *British Journal of Medical Psychology*, 71: 417–445.

Dryden, W. (2009) *Rational Emotive Behaviour Therapy: Distinctive Features*. London: Routledge.

Dugnan, D., Trower, P. and Gilbert, P. (2002) "Measuring vulnerability to threats to self construction: The self and other scale", *Psychology and Psychotherapy: Theory Research and Practice*, 75: 279–294.

Dunkley, D. M., Zuroff, D. C. and Blankstein, K. R. (2006) "Specific perfectionism components versus self-criticism in predicting maladjustment", *Personality and Individual Differences*, 40: 665–676.

Dykman, B. M. (1998) "Integrating cognitive and motivational factors in depression: Initial tests of a goal orientation approach", *Journal of Personality and Social Psychology*, 74: 139–158.

Eells, T. D. (2007) *Handbook of Psychotherapy Case Formulation*, 2nd edn. New York: Guilford Press.

Ellenberger, H. F. (1970) *The Discovery of the Unconscious. The History and Evolution of Dynamic Psychiatry*. New York: Basic Books.

Elliott, R., Watson, J. C., Goldman, R. N. and Greenberg, L. S. (2003) *Learning Emotion-Focused Therapy*. Washington, DC: American Psychological Association.

Fehr, C., Sprecher, S. and Underwood, L. G. (2009) *The Science of Compassionate Love: Theory Research and Application*. Chichester, UK: Wiley.

Field, T. (2000) *Touch Therapy*. New York: Churchill Livingstone.

Fisher, P. and Wells, A. (2009) *Metacognitive Therapy*. London: Routledge.

Fogel, A., Melson, G. F. and Mistry, J. (1986) "Conceptualising the determinants of nurturance: A reassessment of sex differences", in A. Fogel and G. F. Melson (eds), *Origins of Nurturance: Developmental, Biological and Cultural Perspectives on Caregiving* (pp. 53–67). Hillsdale, NJ: Lawrence Erlbaum Associates, Inc.

Frederick, C. and McNeal, S. (1999) *Inner Strengths: Contemporary Psychotherapy and Hypnosis for Ego Strengthening*. Mahwah, NJ: Lawrence Erlbaum Associates, Inc.

Fredrickson, B. L., Cohn, M. A., Coffey, K. A., Pek, J. and Finkel, S. A. (2008) "Open hearts build lives: Positive emotions, induced through loving-kindness mediation, build consequential personal resources", *Journal of Personality and Social Psychology*, 95: 1045–1062.

Gerhardt, S. (2004) *Why Love Matters: How Affection Shapes a Baby's Brain*. London: Routledge.

Germer, C. (2009) *The Mindful Path to Self-Compassion: Freeing your Self from Destructive Thoughts and Emotions*. New York: Guilford Press.

Gibb, B. E., Abramson, L. Y. and Alloy, L. R. (2004) "Emotional maltreatment from parent, verbal peer victimization, and cognitive vulnerability to depression", *Cognitive Therapy and Research*, 28: 1–21.

Gilbert, P. (1984) *Depression: From Psychology to Brain State*. London: Lawrence Erlbaum Associates, Inc.

Gilbert, P. (1989) *Human Nature and Suffering*. Hove, UK: Lawrence Erlbaum Associates, Inc.

Gilbert, P. (1992) *Depression: The Evolution of Powerlessness*. Hove, UK: Lawrence Erlbaum Associates, Inc., and New York: Guilford Press.

Gilbert, P. (1993) "Defence and safety: Their function in social behaviour and psychopathology", *British Journal of Clinical Psychology*, 32: 131–153.

Gilbert, P. (1995) "Biopsychosocial approaches and evolutionary theory as aids to integration in clinical psychology and psychotherapy", *Clinical Psychology and Psychotherapy*, 2: 135–156.

Gilbert, P. (1997) "The evolution of social attractiveness and its role in shame, humiliation, guilt and therapy", *British Journal of Medical Psychology*, 70: 113–147.

Gilbert, P. (1998) "The evolved basis and adaptive functions of cognitive distortions", *British Journal of Medical Psychology*, 71: 447–464.

Gilbert, P. (2000a) "Social mentalities: Internal 'social' conflicts and the role of inner warmth and compassion in cognitive therapy", in P. Gilbert and K. G. Bailey (eds), *Genes on the Couch: Explorations in Evolutionary Psychotherapy* (pp. 118–150). Hove, UK: Brunner-Routledge.

Gilbert, P. (2000b) *Overcoming Depression: A Self-Guide Using Cognitive Behavioural Techniques*, rev. edn. London: Robinsons, and New York: Oxford University Press.

Gilbert, P. (2001a) "Evolutionary approaches to psychopathology: The role of natural defences", *Australian and New Zealand Journal of Psychiatry*, 35: 17–27.

Gilbert, P. (2001b) "Depression and stress: A biopsychosocial exploration of evolved functions and mechanisms", *Stress: The International Journal of the Biology of Stress*, 4: 121–135.

Gilbert, P. (2002) "Evolutionary approaches to psychopathology and cognitive therapy", in P. Gilbert (ed.), Special Edition: Evolutionary Psychology and Cognitive Therapy, *Cognitive Psychotherapy: An International Quarterly*, 16: 263–294.

Gilbert, P. (2003) "Evolution, social roles, and differences in shame and guilt", *Social Research: An International Quarterly of the Social Sciences*, 70: 1205–1230.

Gilbert, P. (ed.) (2004) *Evolutionary Theory and Cognitive Therapy*. New York: Springer.

Gilbert, P. (2005a) "Compassion and cruelty: A biopsychosocial approach", in P. Gilbert (ed.), *Compassion: Conceptualisations, Research and Use in Psychotherapy* (pp. 9–74). London: Routledge.

Gilbert, P. (2005b) "Social mentalities: A biopsychosocial and evolutionary reflection on social relationships", in M. W. Baldwin (ed.), *Interpersonal Cognition* (pp. 299–335). New York: Guilford Press.

Gilbert, P. (ed.) (2005c) *Compassion: Conceptualisations, Research and Use in Psychotherapy*. London: Routledge.

Gilbert, P. (2007a) *Psychotherapy and Counselling for Depression*, 3rd edn. London: Sage.

Gilbert, P. (2007b) "Evolved minds and compassion in the therapeutic relationship", in P. Gilbert and R. Leahy (eds), *The Therapeutic Relationship in the Cognitive Behavioural Psychotherapies* (pp. 106–142). London: Routledge.

Gilbert, P. (2007c) "The evolution of shame as a marker for relationship security", in J. L. Tracy, R. W. Robins and J. P. Tangney
(eds), *The Self-Conscious Emotions: Theory and Research* (pp. 283–
309). New York: Guilford Press.

Gilbert, P. (2007d) *Overcoming Depression: Talks with your Therapist*,
CD (with exercises). London: Constable Robinson.

Gilbert, P. (2009a) *The Compassionate Mind*. London: Constable &
Robinson, and Oaklands, CA: New Harbinger.

Gilbert, P. (2009b) *Overcoming Depression*, 3rd edn. London:
Constable & Robinson, and New York: Basic Books.

Gilbert, P. (2009c) "Evolved minds and compassion-focused imagery
in depression", in L. Stopa (ed.), *Imagery and the Threatened Self:
Perspectives on Mental Imagery and the Self in Cognitive Therapy*
(pp. 206–231). London: Routledge.

Gilbert, P., Broomhead, C., Irons, C., McEwan, K., Bellew, R., Mills,
A., et al. (2007) "Striving to avoid inferiority: Scale development
and its relationship to depression, anxiety and stress", *British
Journal of Social Psychology*, 46: 633–648.

Gilbert, P., Clarke, M., Kempel, S., Miles, J. N. V. and Irons, C.
(2004a) "Criticizing and reassuring oneself: An exploration of forms
style and reasons in female students", *British Journal of Clinical
Psychology*, 43: 31–50.

Gilbert, P., Gilbert, J. and Irons, C. (2004b) "Life events, entrapments
and arrested anger in depression", *Journal of Affective Disorders*, 79:
149–160.

Gilbert, P., Gilbert, J. and Sanghera, J. (2004c) "A focus group
exploration of the impact of izzat, shame, subordination and
entrapment on mental health and service use in South Asian women
living in Derby", *Mental Health, Religion and Culture*, 7: 109–130.

Gilbert, P. and Irons, C. (2004) "A pilot exploration of the use of
compassionate images in a group of self-critical people", *Memory*,
12: 507–516.

Gilbert, P. and Irons, C. (2005) "Focused therapies and compassionate
mind training for shame and self-attacking", in P. Gilbert (ed.),
Compassion: Conceptualisations, Research and Use in Psychotherapy
(pp. 263–325). London: Routledge.

Gilbert, P. and Leahy, R. (eds) (2007) *The Therapeutic Relationship in
the Cognitive Behavioural Psychotherapies*. London: Routledge.

Gilbert, P., McEwan, K., Mitra, R., Franks, L., Richter, A. and
Rockliff, H. (2008) "Feeling safe and content: A specific affect
regulation system? Relationship to depression, anxiety, stress and
self-criticism", *Journal of Positive Psychology*, 3: 182–191.

Gilbert, P. and McGuire, M. (1998) "Shame, social roles and status:

The psycho-biological continuum from monkey to human", in P. Gilbert and B. Andrews (eds), *Shame: Interpersonal Behavior, Psychopathology and Culture* (pp. 99–125). New York: Oxford University Press.

Gilbert, P. and Procter, S. (2006) "Compassionate mind training for people with high shame and self-criticism: A pilot study of a group therapy approach", *Clinical Psychology and Psychotherapy*, 13: 353–379.

Gillath, O., Shaver, P. R. and Mikulincer, M. (2005) "An attachment-theoretical approach to compassion and altruism", in P. Gilbert (ed.), *Compassion: Conceptualisations, Research and Use in Psychotherapy* (pp. 121–147). London: Routledge.

Glasser, A. (2005) *A Call to Compassion: Bringing Buddhist Practices of the Heart into the Soul of Psychotherapy*. Berwick, ME: Nicolas-Hays.

Goss, K. and Gilbert, P. (2002) "Eating disorders, shame and pride: A cognitive-behavioural functional analysis", in P. Gilbert and J. Miles (eds), *Body Shame: Conceptualisation, Research & Treatment* (pp. 219–255). London: Brunner-Routledge.

Gray, J. A. (1987) *The Psychology of Fear and Stress*, 2nd edn. London: Weidenfeld & Nicolson.

Greenberg, L. S., Rice, L. N. and Elliott, R. (1993) *Facilitating Emotional Change: The Moment-by-Moment Process*. New York: Guilford Press.

Hackmann, A. (2005) "Compassionate imagery in the treatment of early memories in axis I anxiety disorders", in P. Gilbert (ed.), *Compassion: Conceptualisations, Research and Use in Psychotherapy* (pp. 352–368). London: Brunner-Routledge.

Haidt, J. (2001) "The emotional dog and its rational tail: A social intuitionist approach to moral judgment", *Psychological Review*, 108: 814–834.

Hall, E., Hall, C., Stradling, P. and Young, D. (2006) *Guided Imagery: Creative Interventions in Counselling and Psychotherapy*. London: Sage.

Hassin, R. R., Uleman, J. S. and Bargh, J. A. (2005) *The New Unconscious*. New York: Oxford University Press.

Hayes, S. C., Follette, V. M. and Linehan, M. N. (2004) *Mindfulness and Acceptance: Expanding the Cognitive Behavioral Tradition*. New York: Guilford Press.

Heinrichs, M., Baumgartner, T., Kirschbaum, C. and Ehlert, U. (2003) "Social support and oxytocin interact to suppress cortisol and subjective response to psychosocial stress", *Biological Psychiatry*, 54: 1389–1398.

Hofer, M. A. (1994) "Early relationships as regulators of infant physiology and behavior", *Acta Paediatrica Supplement*, 397: 9–18.

Holt, J. (1990) *How Children Fail*, 2nd rev. edn. London: Penguin Books.

Hrdy, S. B. (2009) *Mothers and Others: The Evolutionary Origins of Mutual Understanding*. Amherst, MA: Harvard University Press.

Hutcherson, C. A., Seppala, E. M. and Gross, J. J. (2008) "Loving-kindness meditation increases social connectedness", *Emotion*, 8: 720–724.

Ivey, A. E. and Ivey, M. B. (2003) *Intentional Interviewing and Counselling: Facilitating Client Change in a Multicultural Society*, 5th edn. Pacific Grove, CA: Brooks/Cole.

Ji-Woong, K., Sung-Eun, K., Jae-Jin, K., Bumseok, J., Chang-Hyun, P., Ae Ree, S., et al. (2009) "Compassionate attitude towards others' suffering activates the mesolimbic neural system", *Neuropsychologia*, 47(10): 2073–2081.

Kabat-Zinn, J. (2005) *Coming to Our Senses: Healing Ourselves and the World Through Mindfulness*: New York: Piatkus.

Katzow, K. and Safran, J. D. (2007) "Recognizing and resolving ruptures in the therapeutic alliance", in P. Gilbert and R. Leahy (eds), *The Therapeutic Relationship in the Cognitive Behavioural Psychotherapies*. London: Routledge.

Kegan, R. (1982) *The Evolving Self: Problem and Process in Human Development*. Cambridge, MA: Harvard University Press.

Klinger, E. (1977) *Meaning and Void*. Minneapolis, MN: University of Minnesota Press.

Knox, J. (2003) *Archetype, Attachment and Analysis*. London: Routledge.

Koren-Karie, N., Oppenheim, D., Dolev, S., Sher, S. and Etzion-Carasso, A. (2002) "Mothers' insightfulness regarding their infants' internal experience: Relations with maternal sensitivity and infant attachment", *Developmental Psychology*, 38: 534–542.

Laithwaite, H., Gumley, A., O'Hanlon, M., Collins, P., Doyle, P., Abraham, L., et al. (2009). Recovery After Psychosis (RAP): A compassion focused programme for individuals residing in high security settings", *Behavioural and Cognitive Psychotherapy*, 37: 511–526.

Lane, R. D. and Schwartz, G. E. (1987) "Levels of emotional awareness: A cognitive-developmental theory and its application to psychopathology", *American Journal of Psychiatry*, 144: 133-143.

Lanzetta, J. T. and Englis, B. G. (1989) "Expectations of co-operation and competition and their effects on observers' vicarious emotional responses", *Journal of Personality and Social Psychology*, 56: 543–554.

Laursen, B., Pulkkinen, L. and Adams, R. (2002) "The antecedents of agreeableness in adulthood", *Developmental Psychology*, 38: 591–603.

Leahy, R. L. (2001) *Overcoming Resistance in Cognitive Therapy*. New York: Guilford Press.

Leahy, R. L. (2002) "A model of emotional schemas", *Cognitive and Behavioral Practice*, 9: 177–171.

Leahy, R. L. (2005) "A social-cognitive model of validation", in P. Gilbert (ed.), *Compassion: Conceptualisations, Research and Use in Psychotherapy* (pp. 195–217). London: Brunner-Routledge.

Leahy, R. L. (2007) "Schematic mismatch in the therapeutic relationship: A social cognitive model", in P. Gilbert and R. Leahy (eds), *The Therapeutic Relationship in the Cognitive Behavioural Psychotherapies* (pp. 229–254). London: Routledge.

Leary, M. R. (2003) *The Curse of the Self: Self-Awareness, Egotism and the Quality of Human Life*. New York: Oxford University Press.

Leary, M. R. and Tangney, J. P. (eds) (2003) *Handbook of Self and Identity* (pp. 367–383). New York: Guilford Press.

Leary, M. R., Tate, E. B., Adams, C. E., Allen, A. B. and Hancock, J. (2007) "Self-compassion and reactions to unpleasant self-relevant events: The implications of treating oneself kindly", *Journal of Personality and Social Psychology*, 92: 887–904.

LeDoux, J. (1998) *The Emotional Brain*. London: Weidenfeld & Nicolson.

Lee, D. A. (2005) "The perfect nurturer: A model to develop a compassionate mind within the context of cognitive therapy", in P. Gilbert (ed.), *Compassion: Conceptualisations, Research and Use in Psychotherapy* (pp. 326–351). London: Brunner-Routledge.

Leighton, T. D. (2003) *Faces of Compassion: Classic Bodhisattva Archetypes and their Modern Expression*. Boston: Wisdom Publications.

Linehan, M. (1993) *Cognitive Behavioral Treatment of Borderline Personality Disorder*. New York: Guilford Press.

Liotti, G. (2000) "Disorganised attachment, models of borderline states and evolutionary psychotherapy", in P. Gilbert and B. Bailey (eds), *Genes on the Couch: Explorations in Evolutionary Psychotherapy* (pp. 232–256). Hove, UK: Brunner-Routledge.

Liotti, G. (2002) "The inner schema of borderline states and its correction during psychotherapy: A cognitive evolutionary approach", *Journal of Cognitive Psychotherapy: An International Quarterly*, 16: 349–365.

Liotti, G. (2007) "Internal models of attachment in the therapeutic relationship", in P. Gilbert and R. Leahy (eds), *The Therapeutic Relationship in the Cognitive Behavioural Psychotherapies* (pp. 143–161). London: Routledge.

Liotti, G. and Gilbert, P. (in press) "Mentalizing motivation and social mentalities: Theoretical considerations and implications for psychotherapy", in A. Gumley (ed.) *Psychology and Psychotherapy* (special edition).

Liotti, G. and Prunetti, E. (2010) "Metacognitive deficits in trauma-related disorders: Contingent on interpersonal motivational contexts?", in G. Dimaggio and P. H. Lysaker (eds), *Metacognitive and Severe Adult Mental Disorders: From Research to Treatment* (pp. 196–214). London: Routledge.

Longe, O., Maratos, F. A., Gilbert, P., Evans, G., Volker, F., Rockliffe, H., et al. (2010). "Having a word with yourself: Neural correlates of self-criticism and self-reassurance", *NeuroImage*, 49: 1849–1856.

Lutz, A., Brefczynski-Lewis, J., Johnstone, T. and Davidson, R. J. (2008) "Regulation of the neural circuitry of emotion by compassion meditation: Effects of the meditative expertise", *Public Library of Science*, 3: 1–5.

MacDonald, J. and Morley, I. (2001) "Shame and non-disclosure: A study of the emotional isolation of people referred for psychotherapy", *British Journal of Medical Psychology*, 74: 1–21.

MacDonald, K. (1992) "Warmth as a developmental construct: An evolutionary analysis", *Child Development*, 63: 753–773.

MacLean, P. (1985) "Brain evolution relating to family, play and the separation call", *Archives of General Psychiatry*, 42: 405–417.

Marks, I. M. (1987) *Fears, Phobias and Rituals: Panic, Anxiety and their Disorders*. Oxford, UK: Oxford University Press.

Martell, C. R., Addis, M. E. and Jacobson, N. S. (2001) *Depression in Context: Strategies for Guided Action*. New York: Norton.

Matos, M. and Pinto-Gouveia, J. (in press) "Shame as trauma memory", *Clinical Psychology and Psychotherapy*.

Mayhew, S. and Gilbert, P. (2008) "Compassionate mind training with people who hear malevolent voices: A case series report", *Clinical Psychology and Psychotherapy*, 15: 113–138.

McClelland, D. C., Atkinson, J. W., Clark, R. H. and Lowell, E. L. (1953) *The Achievement Motive*. New York: Apple-Century-Crofts.

McCrae, R. R. and Costa, P. T. (1989) "The structure of interpersonal traits: Wiggins circumplex and the five factor model", *Journal of Personality and Social Psychology*, 56: 586–596.

McGregor, I. and Marigold, D. C. (2003) "Defensive zeal and the uncertain self: What makes you so sure?", *Journal of Personality and Social Psychology*, 85: 838–852.

Meins, E., Harris-Waller, J. and Lloyd, A. (2008) "Understanding alexithymia: Association with peer attachment style and mind-mindedness", *Personality and Individual Differences*, 45: 146–152.

Mikulincer, M. and Shaver, P. R. (2007) *Attachment in Adulthood: Structure, Dynamics, and Change*. New York: Guilford Press.

Miranda, R. and Andersen, S. M. (2007) "The therapeutic relationship: Implications from social cognition and transference", in P. Gilbert and R. Leahy (eds), *The Therapeutic Relationship in the Cognitive Behavioural Psychotherapies* (pp. 63–89). London: Routledge.

Neely, M. E., Schallert, D. L., Mohammed, S., Roberts, R. M. and Chen, Y. (2009) "Self-kindness when facing stress: The role of self-compassion, goal regulation, and support in college students' well-being", *Motivation and Emotion*, 33: 88–97.

Neff, K. D. (2003a) "Self-compassion: An alternative conceptualization of a healthy attitude toward oneself", *Self and Identity*, 2: 85–102.

Neff, K. D. (2003b) "The development and validation of a scale to measure self-compassion", *Self and Identity*, 2: 223–250.

Neff, K. D., Hsieh, Y. and Dejitterat, K. (2005) "Self-compassion, achievement goals and coping with academic failure", *Self and Identity*, 4: 263–287.

Neff, K. D. and Vonk, R. (2009) "Self-compassion versus global self-esteem: Two different ways of relating to oneself", *Journal of Personality*, 77: 23–50.

Nesse, R. M. and Ellsworth, P. C. (2009) "Evolution, emotions and emotional disorders", *American Psychologist*, 64: 129–139.

Newberg, A. and Waldman, M. R. (2007) *Born to Believe*. New York: Free Press.

Ogden, P., Minton, K. and Pain, C. (2006) *Trauma and the Body: A Sensorimotor Approach to Psychotherapy*. New York: Norton.

Öhman, A., Lundqvist, D. and Esteves, F. (2001) "The face in the crowd revisited: A threat advantage with Schematic Stimuli", *Journal of Personality and Social Psychology*, 80: 381–396.

Ornstein, R. (1986) *Multimind: A New Way of Looking at Human Beings*. London: Macmillan.

Pace, T. W. W., Negi, L. T. and Adame, D. D. (2008) "Effects of compassion mediation on neuroendocrine, innate immune and behavioral response to psychosocial stress", *Psychoneuroendocrinology*, doi: 10. 1016/j. psyneuen. 2008. 08. 011.

Pani, L. (2000) "Is there an evolutionary mismatch between the normal physiology of the human dopaminergic system and current environmental conditions in industrialized countries?", *Molecular Psychiatry*, 5: 467–475.

Panksepp, J. (1998) *Affective Neuroscience*. New York: Oxford University Press.

Pauley, G. and McPherson, S. (in press) "The experience and meaning of compassion and self-compassion for individuals with depression or anxiety", *Psychology and Psychotherapy*.

Pennebaker, J. W. (1997) *Opening Up: The Healing Power of Expressing Emotions*. New York: Guilford Press.

Peterson, C. and Seligman, M. E. (2004) *Character Strengths and Virtues*. New York: Oxford University Press.

Porges, S. (2003) "The polyvagal theory: Phylogenetic contributions to social behaviour", *Physiology & Behavior*, 79: 503–513.

Porges, S. W. (2007) "The polyvagal perspective", *Biological Psychology*, 74: 116–143.

Power, M. and Dalgleish, T. (1997) *Cognition and Emotion: From Order to Disorder*. Hove, UK: Psychology Press.

Quirin, M., Kazen, M. and Kuhl, J. (2009) "When nonsense sounds happy or helpless: The Implicit Positive and Negative Affect Test (IPANAT)", *Journal of Personality and Social Psychology*, 97: 500–516.

Reed 11, A. and Aquino, K. F. (2003) "Moral identity and the expanding circle of moral regard toward out groups", *Journal of Personality and Social Psychology*, 64: 1270–1286.

Rein, G., Atkinson, M. and McCraty, R. (1995) "The physiological and psychological effects of compassion and anger", *Journal for the Advancement of Medicine*, 8: 87–105.

Ricard, M. (2003) *Happiness: A Guide to Developing Life's Most Important Skill*. London: Atlantic Books.

Rockliff, H., Gilbert, P., McEwan, K., Lightman, S. and Glover, D. (2008) "A pilot exploration of heart rate variability and salivary cortisol responses to compassion-focused imagery", *Journal of Clinical Neuropsychiatry*, 5: 132–139.

Rogers, C. (1957) "The necessary and sufficient conditions of therapeutic change", *Journal of Consulting Psychology*, 21: 95–103.

Rohner, R. P. (1986) *The Warmth Dimension: Foundations of Parental Acceptance–Rejection Theory*. Beverly Hills, CA: Sage.

Rohner, R. P. (2004) "The parent 'acceptance–rejection syndrome': Universal correlates of perceived rejection", *American Psychologist*, 59: 830–840.

Rosen, H. (1993) "Developing themes in the field of cognitive therapy", in K. T. Kuehlwein and H. Rosen (eds), *Cognitive*

Therapies in Action: Evolving Innovative Practice (pp. 403–434). San Francisco, CA: Jossey Bass.

Rosen, J. B. and Schulkin, J. (1998) "From normal fear to pathological anxiety", *Psychological Bulletin*, 105: 325–350.

Rowan, J. (1990) *Subpersonalities: The People Inside Us*. London: Routledge.

Rubin, T. I. (1998) *Compassion and Self-Hate: An Alternative to Despair*. New York: Touchstone (Originally published in 1975).

Safran, J. D. and Segal, Z. V. (1990) *Interpersonal Process in Cognitive Therapy*. New York: Basic Books.

Salkovskis, P. M. (1996) "The cognitive approach to anxiety: Threat beliefs, safety-seeking behavior, and the special case of health anxiety and obsessions", in P. M. Salkovskis (ed.), *Frontiers of Cognitive Therapy* (pp. 48–74). New York: Guilford Press.

Salzberg, S. (1995) *Loving-Kindness: The Revolutionary Art of Happiness*. Boston: Shambhala.

Sapolsky, R. M. (1994) *Why Zebras Don't Get Ulcers: An Updated Guide to Stress, Stress-Related Disease, and Coping*. New York: Freeman.

Schore, A. N. (1994) *Affect Regulation and the Origin of the Self: The Neurobiology of Emotional Development*. Hillsdale, NJ: Lawrence Erlbaum Associates, Inc.

Schore, A. N. (2001) "The effects of early relational trauma on right brain development, affect regulation, and infant mental health", *Infant Mental Health Journal*, 22: 201–269.

Segal, Z. V., Williams, J. M. G. and Teasdale, J. (2002) *Mindfulness-Based Cognitive Therapy for Depression: A New Approach to Preventing Relapse*. New York: Guilford Press.

Siegel, D. J. (2001) "Toward an interpersonal neurobiology of the developing mind: Attachment relationships, 'mindsight' and neural integration", *Infant Mental Health Journal*, 22: 67–94.

Siegel, D. J. (2007) *The Mindful Brain: Reflection and Attunement in the Cultivation of Well-Being*. New York: Norton.

Siegel, D. J. (2010) *The Mindful Therapist*. New York: Norton.

Singer, J. L. (2006) *Imagery in Psychotherapy*. Washington, DC: American Psychological Association.

Sloman, L. (2000) "The syndrome of rejection sensitivity: An evolutionary perspective", in P. Gilbert and K. Bailey (eds), *Genes on the Couch: Explorations in Evolutionary Psychotherapy* (pp. 257–275). Hove, UK: Psychology Press.

Stern, D. N. (2004) *The Present Moment in Psychotherapy and Everyday Life*. New York: Norton.

Stevens, A. (1999) *Ariadne's Clue: A Guide to the Symbols of Human-kind*. Princeton, NJ: The Princeton University Press.

Stopa, L. (2009) *Imagery and the Threatened Self: Perspectives on Mental Imagery and the Self in Cognitive Therapy*. London: Routledge.

Stott, R. (2007) "When the head and heart do not agree: A theoretical and clinical analysis of rational–emotional dissociation (RED) in cognitive therapy", *Journal of Cognitive Psychotherapy: An International Quarterly*, 21: 37–50.

Suomi, S. J. (1999) "Attachment in rhesus monkeys", in J. Cassidy and P. R. Shaver (eds), *Handbook of Attachment: Theory, Research and Clinical Applications* (pp. 181–197). New York: Guilford Press.

Swan, S. and Andrews, B. (2003) "The relationship between shame, eating disorders and disclosure in treatment", *British Journal of Clinical Psychology*, 42: 367–378.

Swann, W. B., Rentfrow, P. J. and Guinn, J. (2003) "Self verification: The search for coherence", in M. R. Leary and J. P. Tangney (eds), *Handbook of Self and Identity* (pp. 367–383). New York: Guilford Press.

Synder, C. R. and Ingram, R. E. (2006) "Special issue on positive psychology", *Journal of Cognitive Psychotherapy: An International Quarterly*, 20: 115–240.

Tangney, J. P. and Dearing, R. L. (2002) *Shame and Guilt*. New York: Guilford Press.

Tarrier, N. (ed.) (2006) *Case Formulation in Cognitive Behaviour Therapy: The Treatment of Challenging and Complex Cases*. London: Routledge.

Teasdale, J. D. and Barnard, P. J. (1993) *Affect, Cognition and Change: Remodelling Depressive Affect*. Hove, UK: Psychology Press.

Teicher, M. H. (2002) "Scars that won't heal: The neurobiology of the abused child", *Scientific American*, 286(3): 54–61.

Teicher, M. H., Samson, J. A., Polcari, A. and McGreenery, C. E. (2006) "Sticks and stones and hurtful words: Relative effects of various forms of childhood maltreatment", *American Journal of Psychiatry*, 163: 993–1000.

Thwaites, R. and Freeston, M. H. (2005) "Safety-seeking behaviours: Fact or fiction? How can we clinically differentiate between safety behaviours and additive coping strategies across anxiety disorders?", *Behavioural and Cognitive Psychotherapy*, 33: 177–188.

Tomkins, S. S. (1987) "Script theory", in J. Aronoff, A. I. Rubin and R. A. Zucker (eds), *The Emergence of Personality* (pp. 147–216). New York: Springer.

Tracy, J. L., Robins, R. W. and Tangney, J. P. (eds) (2007) *The Self-*

Conscious Emotions: Theory and Research. New York: Guilford Press.

Trevarthen, C. and Aitken, K. (2001) "Infant intersubjectivity: Research, theory, and clinical applications", *Journal of Child Psychology and Psychiatry*, 42: 3–48.

Twenge, J. M., Gentile, B., DeWall, C. N., Ma, D. S., Lacefield, K. and Schurtz, D. R. (2010) "Birth cohort increases in psychopathology among young Americans, 1938–2007: A cross-temporal meta-analysis of the MMPI", *Clinical Psychology Review*, 30: 145–154.

Vessantara. (1993) *Meeting the Buddhas: A Guide to Buddhas, Bodhisattvas and Tantric Deities.* New York: Winhorse Publications.

Wallin, D. (2007) *Attachment in Psychotherapy.* New York: Guilford Press.

Wang, S. (2005) "A conceptual framework for integrating research related to the physiology of compassion and the wisdom of Buddhist teachings", in P. Gilbert (ed.), *Compassion: Conceptualisations, Research and Use in Psychotherapy* (pp. 75–120). London: Brunner-Routledge.

Warneken, F. and Tomasello, M. (2009) "The roots of altruism", *British Journal of Psychology*, 100: 455–471.

Wells, A. (2000) *Emotional Disorders and Metacognition: Innovative Cognitive Therapy.* Chichester, UK: Wiley.

Wheatley, J., Brewin, C. R., Patel, T., Hackmann, A., Wells, A., Fischer, P., et al. (2007) "I'll believe it when I see it: Imagery rescripting of intrusive sensory memories", *Journal of Behavior Therapy and Experimental Psychiatry*, 39: 371–385.

Whelton, W. J. and Greenberg, L. S. (2005) "Emotion in self-criticism", *Personality and Individual Differences*, 38: 1583–1595.

Wilkinson, R. and Pickett, K. (2009) *The Spirit Level: Why More Equal Societies Almost Always Do Better.* London: Penguin.

Williams, M., Teasdale, J., Segal, Z. and Kabat-Zinn, J. (2007) *The Mindful Way Through Depression: Freeing Yourself From Chronic Unhappiness.* New York: Guilford Press.

Wills, F. (2009) *Beck's Cognitive Therapy: Distinctive Features.* London: Routledge.

Wilson, K. G. (2009) *Mindfulness for Two: An Acceptance and Commitment Therapy Approach to Mindfulness and Psychotherapy.* Oakland, CA: New Harbinger.

Wolfe, R. N., Lennox, R. D. and Cutler, B. L. (1986) "Getting along and getting ahead: Empirical support for a theory of protective and acquisitive self-presentation", *Journal of Social and Personality Psychology*, 50: 356–361.

Wroe, A. L. and Salkovskis, P. M. (2000) "Causing harm and allowing harm: A study of beliefs in obsessional problems", *Behaviour Therapy and Research*, 38: 114–1162.

Zuroff, D. C., Santor, D. and Mongrain, M. (2005) "Dependency, self-criticism, and maladjustment", in J. S. Auerbach, K. N. Levy and C. E. Schaffer (eds), *Relatedness, Self-Definition and Mental Representation: Essays in Honour of Sidney J. Blatt* (pp. 75–90). London: Routledge.

Index

Note: Page numbers in **bold** refer to figures and page numbers in *italic* refer to tables.